The American Culinary Society's
MENU MAKER
Marguerite Patten

The American Culinary Society's
MENU MAKER

Marguerite Patten

CRESCENT BOOKS

This edition first published in 1974 by
CRESCENT BOOKS
a division of Crown Publishers Inc.
by arrangement with Octopus Books Ltd.

ISBN 0 7064 0389 4

© 1973 Octopus Books Limited

Some recipes and illustrations in this book were
published in 'The American Culinary Society's Guide to
Perfect Cooking'

Produced by Mandarin Publishers Limited
14 Westlands Road, Quarry Bay, Hong Kong
Filmset and printed in Hong Kong

Contents

Introduction

This is a book of complete menus for many different occasions and requirements. As you will see from the Contents on page 5, they range from Celebration Meals of all kinds to menus for the days when the housekeeping budget is at its lowest. I have also included suggestions for Slimming Meals and some that pay special attention to Health-giving Foods, so if you, or a member of your family, are over-weight or seem less fit than usual, these meals should help to solve the problems.
In many cases I have suggested dishes that are a good basis for variation, so that after you have tried the recipe as written, you can alter the flavorings, or use a different meat, fish or fruit.
I hope you enjoy using these menus and that they will provide your family and friends with pleasurable meals, while allowing you, the cook, to relax a little when it comes to the ever-present problem of 'what shall we have to eat?'.

Marguerite Patten

Marguerite Patten

Aids When Planning Meals

Shopping takes a great deal of time and effort, so it is wise to have a well-stocked larder, refrigerator and home freezer. If you choose the foods carefully you can plan menus over several days without shopping.

Your staple cupboard
Naturally you will have supplies of flour, sugars (granulated, brown sugar for richer cakes, confectioners' sugar for decorating cakes), tea and coffee, but make sure you have:
rice – long grain for savory dishes, such as Paella, see page 100, and to serve with various savory dishes.
pasta – spaghetti, etc., for quick and economical dishes, see page 16.
dehydrated herbs – if you do not grow your own fresh herbs.
dehydrated vegetables – these take up little space; modern dried peas and beans do not need prolonged soaking. Dehydrated potatoes enable you to make mashed potatoes and other savory dishes very quickly and easily. Dehydrated onion saves the bother of chopping the fresh vegetable if a little flavoring is needed.
spices and flavorings
sauces – such as soy, and Worcestershire.
canned soups – choose some of the unusual ones and those that could be used for sauces.
canned meats – tongue, ham, pork and ham are all useful; see pages 18 and 22.
canned fish – sardines, tuna, salmon can all be turned into interesting dishes, see pages 16 and 18.
canned fruit – can be served by itself or it can form part of an interesting dessert, see pages 20, 26 and 47.
canned cream and/or evaporated milk and dehydrated milk – be sure you are never short of these valuable foods.
root vegetables – store in a cool place; use them in rotation, otherwise potatoes become green and carrots shrivel up.
citrus fruits keep well in a cool place.

Your refrigerator
Use your refrigerator in a sensible manner; do not expect perishable foods to keep more than a few days, check that you use items such as butter in the order in which it was purchased. It is all too easy to bring in fresh supplies, use these first and still have old stocks. Naturally you will use much of your refrigerator space for meat and fish, and for left-over foods you plan to use up within a day or two, but in addition check you have:
butter, margarine and other fats – these keep well. Oil does not need keeping in the refrigerator, it can be stored in a cupboard.
cheese – the true strong cooking cheese, Parmesan, need not be stored in the refrigerator; it can be purchased ready-grated or grate your own and keep in a screw-topped container. Store Gruyère, Cheddar and hard cheeses in the refrigerator; cover well, to prevent drying. Never waste dry pieces of Cheddar or similar cheese, grate and use in cooking. Brie, Camembert and Stilton are better if kept in a cupboard at room temperature.
fresh parsley and other herbs and salad ingredients – these keep well in covered containers in the refrigerator.
bacon – wrap or buy in polythene bags (note the date by which the bacon must be used). Keep adequate stocks so you can use this for quick savory dishes, see page 16.

Your home freezer
Use this as a supermarket in your own home. Keep a clear record of just what is in the cabinet and where it has been placed and label packages of food clearly, so there is no problem of finding them, and so you can keep a good idea of your 'stock'. In addition to making up dishes to keep in the freezer for emergencies, these are some of the useful frozen foods to store:
vegetables and fruits – excellent for all purposes.
meat – steaks, chops and smaller pieces of meat can be cooked from the frozen state, so can jointed raw chicken. Whole poultry and joints should be defrosted before using.
fish – ready-coated for frying, shell fish, etc.
bread, cakes, scones – sliced bread can be toasted from the frozen state and rolls need just a few minutes warming through.
ice cream – home- or commercially-made which can be bought in bulk.

Money Saving Meals

Many good foods are inexpensive to buy and you will find a selection of interesting dishes that form appetizing, as well as cheap, meals in the next pages. Be selective about shopping, choose foods that are in season, for those out of season are always more expensive and often not at their best.

Learn about the cheaper meats, stewing steak, ground beef (excellent for meat sauces, loaves, hamburgers), neck and breast of lamb.

Choose some of the inexpensive white fish and 'dress it up' with flavorsome sauces. Buy in larger quantities where practicable and save money that way. All menus in this chapter serve 4–6.

GARBURE (BEAN SOUP)

1 or 2 slices bacon · 2 tablespoons fat · 1 large onion ·
1 clove garlic (optional) · 2 carrots ·
1½ cups beef or chicken stock or water and bouillon
cubes · 1 medium-sized can haricot beans ·
Topping: chopped parsley, grated cheese

Chop the bacon and fry lightly for a few minutes. Lift out of
the pan, add the fat to the bacon fat in the pan and heat.
Chop the onion, crush the garlic, if used. Fry the onion and
garlic until soft, but not brown. Add the chopped or grated
carrots and stock or water and bouillon cubes. Simmer for
15 minutes, add beans and bacon. Serve topped with parsley
and cheese.

DEVILED COD

¼ cup margarine or butter ·
1–2 teaspoons curry powder ·
1 teaspoon Worcestershire sauce ·
1–2½ tablespoons white raisins ·
1 tablespoon sweet chutney · good shake pepper ·
pinch salt · 4 tablespoons fresh breadcrumbs ·
4 or 6 portions of cod ·
Garnish: lemon, watercress

Grease an oven-proof dish with 1 tablespoon margarine or
butter. Melt the remainder, and blend with the curry powder,
Worcestershire sauce, raisins and chutney. Add the pepper
and salt, mix well, then stir the breadcrumbs into the mixture.
Spread over the top of the fish and bake, uncovered, for
approximately 25 minutes in a moderately hot oven, 400°F.
Garnish and serve with salad.

LEMON APPLE MERINGUE PIE

short crust pastry, made with 1½ cups flour, etc.
(see page 71) · 2 really large cooking apples ·
grated rind and juice 1 lemon ·
¾ cup sugar · 2 eggs

Line a 7–8-inch flan case with the pastry. Bake 'blind'.
Meanwhile, peel, slice and cook the apples with the lemon
rind and juice and ¼ cup sugar until a thick pulp. Beat until
smooth. Separate the egg yolks from the whites. Add the
beaten egg yolks to the apple mixture. Spoon into the pastry
case. Beat the egg whites until very stiff, then very gradually
beat in ½ cup sugar. Either bake for about 25–30 minutes in
a very moderate oven, 325°F and serve hot, or bake for about
1 hour in a very slow oven, 275°F, and serve cold.

Garbure, Deviled Cod, Salad, Lemon Apple Meringue Pie

STEAK UPSIDE DOWN PIE

2 onions · 2–3 tomatoes ·
a few mushrooms or mushroom stalks ·
¼ cup butter or margarine ·
1¼ cups stock or water and a bouillon cube ·
¾ lb. ground beef · seasoning ·
Topping: 1½ cups self-rising flour · seasoning ·
¼ cup fat · ½ cup grated Cheddar cheese ·
1 egg yolk · milk
Garnish : parsley sprigs

Chop the vegetables and fry in the butter or margarine until soft. Add the stock or water and bouillon cube and the ground beef. Stir until a smooth, thick mixture, season well, cook for 15 minutes only in an uncovered pan, stir from time to time. Meanwhile, prepare the topping. Sift the flour with seasoning. Rub in the fat, add the grated cheese – this is an excellent way to use stale pieces. Bind with the egg yolk and milk to make a soft rolling consistency. Form into a 7–8-inch round. Put the meat mixture into a cake pan (without a loose base) or oven-proof dish, top with the dough. Bake in the centre of a moderate oven, 350–375°F, for about 50 minutes. Invert on to a hot dish and garnish with parsley sprigs.

CREAMED CARROTS

1 lb. carrots · 1 tablespoon butter or margarine ·
1–2½ tablespoons milk · grated nutmeg · seasoning ·
Garnish: chopped parsley

Cook carrots and mash with butter or margarine, milk, a little nutmeg and plenty of seasoning. Top with parsley.

LYONNAISE POTATOES

1 lb. cooked potatoes · about ½ lb. onions ·
¼ cup butter · chopped parsley

Slice the potatoes fairly thickly. Slice the onions very thinly. Heat the butter in a pan and cook the onions until nearly tender. Add the potatoes and mix well, then heat gently until pale golden. Top with chopped parsley before serving.

GRAPE AND ORANGE WHIP

2–3 very large oranges ·
1 package orange-flavored gelatin ·
2½–4 tablespoons heavy cream · 1 egg white ·
skinned de-seeded grapes ·
few whole or halved grapes

Halve the oranges carefully. Squeeze out the juice, but try to keep the orange cases intact. Measure the juice and add enough hot water to give just 2 cups. Dissolve the gelatin in this and allow to cool, then begin to stiffen slightly. Beat briskly then fold in the cream and stiffly beaten egg white (left from the main dish). Put a layer of skinned de-seeded grapes at the bottom of each orange case, top with the gelatin mixture and decorate with whole or halved grapes when set.

Steak Upside Down Pie with Creamed Carrots and Lyonnaise Potatoes, Grape and Orange Whip

MENU

GOLDEN CHEESE SOUP
MILANAISE KIDNEYS WITH NOODLES
CAULIFLOWER POLONAISE
HONEY BANANA CREAMS

GOLDEN CHEESE SOUP

¼ cup margarine or butter · ½ cup flour · 1¼ cups milk ·
2 cups chicken stock or water and a bouillon cube ·
2 carrots, grated · 1½ cups Cheddar cheese, grated ·
Topping: chopped parsley or watercress leaves

Heat the margarine or butter in a pan, stir in the flour and
cook gently for several minutes. Gradually stir in the milk
and chicken stock or water and bouillon cube. Bring to the
boil, stir well until thickened. Add the grated carrots, cook
for a few minutes only, then add the grated cheese. Heat until
melted. Pour into soup cups, top with chopped parsley or
watercress.

MILANAISE KIDNEYS

2–3 onions, thinly sliced ·
about 4 large tomatoes, skinned and thickly sliced ·
fat for frying · approximately ½ cup stock ·
about 7 lambs' kidneys, halved · seasoning ·
1–2 teaspoons cornstarch ·
few tablespoons extra stock or dry red wine ·
Garnish: fried bits of bacon

Fry the onions and tomatoes in a little fat until soft. Add the
stock and lambs' kidneys. Season well and simmer steadily
in a covered pan for about 10–15 minutes. Blend the cornstarch with the extra stock or wine. Stir into the mixture
and continue stirring until thick. Garnish with bacon.

CAULIFLOWER POLONAISE

1 cauliflower · 1½ tablespoons fresh breadcrumbs ·
1 tablespoon margarine ·
2 tablespoons chopped parsley · 1 hard-cooked egg

Break the cauliflower into pieces. Cook until just tender,
strain, then arrange neatly in a serving dish. Fry the breadcrumbs in the margarine, add the chopped parsley and
finally the chopped egg. Spoon over the cauliflower.

HONEY BANANA CREAMS

3 large ripe bananas · 1 large lemon ·
3 tablespoons honey · 1¼ cups milk ·
1 envelope unflavored gelatin · ½ cup water ·
3 tablespoons heavy cream, whipped ·
ice cream or cream

Mash the bananas with the lemon juice. Heat the honey in
the milk, stir into the mashed bananas. Soften the gelatin in
3 tablespoons of the cold water. Simmer the lemon rind in
the remainder of the water for 5–6 minutes to extract the
maximum flavor. Strain, then blend the liquid with the
softened gelatin. Stir until gelatin is dissolved. When quite
clear add to the banana mixture. Allow to cool and stiffen
very slightly then fold in the lightly whipped cream. Spoon
into glasses. Serve topped with ice cream or whipped cream.

Honey Banana Creams

2–3 tablespoons chopped gherkins ·
1 teaspoon liquid from gherkins ·
1–2 teaspoons chopped fresh herbs · 1 egg ·
chicken stock ·
Garnish: watercress

Simmer the chicken giblets in a little water to make some
stock. Blend the sausagemeat with the rest of the ingredients.
To give a moist texture to the stuffing add a little giblet stock.
Put the stuffing into the chicken and weigh. Allow 15 minutes
per lb. and 15 minutes over in a moderately hot to hot oven,
400–425°F. Cover the chicken breast with fat to keep it
moist during cooking. If preferred wrap in foil, but allow
30 minutes longer cooking time and open the foil for the last
30 minutes to brown the bird. Serve with thickened gravy,
from the giblet stock. If you wish to give this a slightly sweet
sour flavor, add 2 teaspoons honey and a squeeze of lemon
juice after it has thickened. Serve with roast potatoes and
cooked corn and garnish with watercress.

APPLE AND DATE CHARLOTTE

6 slices bread · margarine or butter ·
about 1 lb. cooking apples · 2½–4 tablespoons sugar ·
¾ cup chopped dates · cinnamon · brown sugar

Spread the bread with the margarine or butter, remove the
crusts if desired. Cut the slices of bread into fingers. Simmer
the peeled sliced apples in the minimum of water, adding the
sugar. When soft add the dates and a sprinkling of powdered
cinnamon to taste. Sprinkle the bottom of a pie dish with a
little brown sugar. Put half the fingers of bread in the dish
with the buttered side down so it will brown and crisp.
Cover with the apple mixture, then the rest of the slices of
bread and butter, this time the buttered side uppermost.
Sprinkle lightly with brown sugar. Bake for about 10–15
minutes, then leave in the oven when removing the chicken,
but lower the heat to very moderate, 325°F.

MENU
SOUFFLÉ EGGS
ROAST CHICKEN WITH SWEET
SOUR STUFFING
ROAST POTATOES AND CORN
APPLE AND DATE CHARLOTTE

SOUFFLÉ EGGS

4 eggs · 2 tablespoons butter ·
2 tablespoons light cream · seasoning ·
½ cup chopped cooked ham or grated cheese

Separate the egg yolks from the whites, beat the whites until
stiff. Butter individual oven-proof shallow dishes. Beat the
yolks with the cream, season well, mix with tiny pieces of
ham or grated cheese and fold into the whites. Put into the
dishes and bake for 10 minutes towards the top of a moderately
hot to hot oven, 400–425°F. Serve at once.

ROAST CHICKEN WITH SWEET SOUR
STUFFING

4½ lb. roasting chicken with giblets · water ·
1 lb. sausagemeat · 2½–4 tablespoons seedless raisins ·
2½–4 tablespoons chopped walnuts ·

Above: Roast Chicken with Sweet Sour Stuffing, Roast Potatoes and Cooked Corn

Opposite page: Apple and Date Charlotte

This menu provides a buffet or formal meal for 6 people at a reasonable cost.

AVOCADO COCKTAIL

I grapefruit · I ripe avocado ·
¼ cup shelled small shrimp · little mayonnaise · lettuce

Cut away the peel and pith from the grapefruit and remove the fruit segments. Put 6 segments on one side for garnish. Cut the remainder into small pieces and put into a bowl. Halve the avocado, remove the pit, skin and slice the fruit. Mix with the grapefruit pieces, shrimp and a little mayonnaise. Arrange a little finely shredded lettuce in individual glasses or on small dishes, top with the avocado and shrimp mixture and garnish with the reserved grapefruit segments.

HAM AND MUSHROOM FLAN

short crust pastry made with 2 cups flour, etc.
(see page 71) · 3 tablespoons margarine ·
6 tablespoons flour · 2 cups milk · ½ lb. cooked ham ·
6 tablespoons grated cheese · seasoning ·
12 button mushrooms · 2 tablespoons butter or fat

Make the pastry, roll out and make a 9–10-inch flan case.

Peach and Cherry Trifle

Bake 'blind' until crisp and golden brown. Meanwhile, make a white sauce with the margarine, flour and milk, see recipe page 15. Add the neatly diced ham, grated cheese, and seasoning. Heat for a few minutes only. Fry the mushrooms in the butter or fat. Fill the *hot* pastry case with the *hot* ham mixture. Top with the cooked mushrooms and serve.

CUCUMBER AND TOMATO SALAD

watercress · cucumber · tomatoes · seasoning ·
vinegar or lemon juice · chives or scallions

Put a layer of watercress into a shallow dish. Arrange thin slices of cucumber and tomato over this. Flavor with salt, pepper, a little vinegar or lemon juice and chopped chives or scallions.

PEACH AND CHERRY TRIFLE

I package (3¼ oz.) vanilla pudding mix ·
lemon or orange rind · jelly roll or sponge cake · jam
I–2 sliced fresh peaches or I can (16 oz.) peaches
Decoration: I or 2 fresh peaches · lemon juice ·
½ cup heavy cream, lightly whipped ·
glacé or fresh cherries

Make the pudding according to instructions on the package, but put thin strips of lemon or orange rind into the milk and remove when the vanilla pudding has thickened. Arrange 6 slices of jelly roll or sponge cake, split and spread with jam, in a serving dish. Top with the sliced fresh peaches or half of the drained canned peaches. Spoon the hot pudding over the sponge and fruit and allow to cool. Decorate with the thinly sliced fresh peaches (dipped in lemon juice) or the remainder of the canned fruit, the whipped cream and cherries.

Grapefruit and Melon Cocktails

┌─────────────────────────────────────┐

MENU

GRAPEFRUIT AND MELON COCKTAILS
CHICKEN STUFFED PANCAKES AU GRATIN
CELERY COLESLAW
CARAMEL CRUMB CUSTARD

└─────────────────────────────────────┘

GRAPEFRUIT AND MELON COCKTAILS
This is an excellent way of using part of a melon.

¼ cup sugar · ½ cup water · 1 tablespoon sherry ·
little ground ginger ·
2 large grapefruit, peeled and sectioned ·
½ small melon, diced

Make a syrup by boiling together the sugar and water. Flavor with the sherry and ginger. Combine the grapefruit with the melon. Put into glasses. Spoon over the syrup and chill.

CHICKEN STUFFED PANCAKES AU GRATIN
This is a good way to use left-over pieces of chicken.

8–12 pancakes (see page 16) ·
2 cups white sauce (see below) ·
small pieces of cooked chicken · stuffing ·
½ chopped green or red pepper · little cooked corn ·
fresh breadcrumbs · little grated cheese ·
little margarine or butter

Cook the pancakes as the recipe on page 16. Make a creamy white sauce (see below), using a little chicken stock for flavoring the sauce. Mix half of this with small pieces of

cooked chicken, tiny pieces of stuffing, if available, chopped green or red pepper and a little cooked corn. Fill the pancakes with this, then put into an oven-proof dish. Spoon over the remaining sauce, breadcrumbs and a little grated cheese. Top with margarine or butter and heat for about 25 minutes in a moderately hot oven, 375–400°F. Serve at once.

To make white sauce: Heat 3 tablespoons butter in a pan, stir in 6 tablespoons flour and cook for 2–3 minutes. Add 2 scant cups milk, bring to the boil, stirring or beating well until smooth. Cook until thickened, then season.

CELERY COLESLAW

½ small cabbage, shredded ·
few sticks raw celery, chopped · little mayonnaise ·
few gherkins · few capers

Toss the finely shredded cabbage and finely chopped celery in the mayonnaise. Add chopped gherkin and capers.

CARAMEL CRUMB CUSTARD

1 package (3¼ oz.) vanilla pudding mix ·
plain sponge cake ·
little fruit juice, sherry or white wine ·
cooked apples or other fresh or cooked fruit ·
caramel (see page 16)

Make the pudding according to the directions on the package. Dice the sponge cake and put into individual glasses. Moisten with a very little fruit juice, sherry or white wine, then top with sliced cooked apples or other fruit. Spoon the warm pudding over the top and allow it to cool. Meanwhile, make the caramel as page 16. When the sugar mixture is brown pour it on to a tin and let it set. Crush with a rolling pin and sprinkle over the top of each dessert.

SPAGHETTI WITH BACON AND ONION

½ lb. spaghetti · seasoning · 6 slices bacon ·
3 large onions, chopped or grated · chopped parsley ·
grated cheese

Cook the spaghetti in seasoned boiling water until nearly tender. Chop the bacon and fry for 2–3 minutes; add the chopped or grated onions and cook steadily. Drain the spaghetti and return to the pan, add the bacon and onions and as much parsley and cheese as desired. Serve immediately.

GRILLED COD STEAKS

4 cod steaks · seasoning · juice ½ lemon ·
¼ cup butter or margarine · Garnish: 1 lemon, parsley

Season the fish and flavor with the lemon juice. Melt the butter or margarine. Brush either the grid of the broiling pan, or a piece of foil spread over the grid of the broiling pan (this saves time in washing-up) with butter or margarine. Put the fish on the grid or foil, brush with butter or margarine and broil quickly for 2–3 minutes. Turn and broil quickly for the same time on the other side, then lower the heat and cook for a few more minutes until the cod is tender. Lift on to a hot dish, top with the parsley butter (see below) and garnish with sliced lemon and parsley.

PARSLEY BUTTER

Cream ¼ cup butter or margarine with seasoning, the finely grated rind and juice of ½ lemon and 1–2½ tablespoons chopped parsley. Cut into 4 neat slices or form into 4 rounds. Chill well and put on the fish before serving.
To vary: Add 1 tablespoon chopped fresh dill or a good pinch of the dried herb in place of the parsley. Add the lemon juice as above.

CARAMELED APPLES

½ cup sugar · ½ cup water · 4 dessert apples

For the caramel sauce, put the sugar and 5 tablespoons water into a heavy pan, stir until the sugar has dissolved, then boil *without stirring* until golden brown. Add the rest of the water and blend with the caramel. Peel, core and slice the apples, put into a dish, add the warm caramel then allow to cool. Turn over once or twice so the apples absorb the sauce.

TUNA PANCAKES

Pancakes: 1 cup flour · pinch salt · 1 egg ·
1¼ cups milk or milk and water · fat for frying ·
Filling: 1 medium-sized can tuna · scant 1¼ cups milk ·
2 tablespoons margarine · 1 onion · ¼ cup flour ·
2½ tablespoons chopped parsley · seasoning

Sift together the flour and salt and add the egg and milk, then beat until a smooth batter. Heat a little fat in the pan, pour in enough batter to give a thin coating, fry for 2 minutes, turn and fry on the second side. Lift on to a heat-proof dish and top with a little filling. Keep hot in the oven and make layers of pancakes and filling. To make the filling, flake the fish, add any liquid from the can to the milk. Heat the margarine and fry the chopped onion for 3–4 minutes, blend the flour and liquid and stir into the onion, continue stirring until thickened. Add the rest of the ingredients.
To vary: Add tiny pieces of lemon pulp, diced cucumber, chopped hard-cooked egg, etc., to the tuna.

SARDINE FRITTERS

1 small can sardines in oil · juice ½ lemon · seasoning ·
6 large slices of bread · 2 tablespoons butter ·
Coating: 1 egg · 2½ tablespoons milk ·
For frying: 2 tablespoons cooking fat

Drain, bone and mash the sardines with lemon juice and plenty of seasoning. Cut the crusts from the bread, spread with butter; do not be too generous, since sardines are very oily fish. Sandwich the bread with the mashed sardines, cut into about 12 fingers. Beat the egg and milk, dip the fingers in this. Put any oil from the can of sardines into the pan plus the fat. Heat gently until the fat has melted, then fry the sardine fingers until crisp and brown on either side. Drain on absorbent paper and serve at once.

CHEF'S SALAD

This is not only a good picnic dish, see page 68, but an economical one too. Serve with canned or freshly cooked new potatoes.

Spaghetti with Bacon and Onion

Time Saving Menus

The very large range of convenience foods available means that good meals, interesting meals and nutritious meals can be prepared within minutes.
Canned Foods Meat, fish, fruit and vegetables all add variety to a menu and the food needs little, if any, heating.
Frozen Foods These have caused a mild 'revolution' in our kitchens.
Fresh 'Convenience Foods' Cooked meats, cheese, milk, bread and many fruits and vegetables can be termed 'convenience foods', for they can provide the basis of speedy and interesting meals.
All menus in this chapter serve 4.

MENU

DANISH KEBABS
WITH MUSTARD SAUCE
AND GREEN SALAD
ORANGE CONDÉ
CHEESE WAFERS

MENU

CHICKEN BORSCH
SARDINES NIÇOISE
CELERY CHEESE BISCUITS
CHEESE AND FRESH FRUIT

DANISH KEBABS WITH MUSTARD SAUCE

1 can (12 oz.) luncheon meat or ham ·
1 small can cocktail frankfurters ·
1 small can or tube pâté · 4–8 firm tomatoes ·
2 tablespoons margarine or butter ·
Sauce: 1 can (10½ oz.) chicken broth, undiluted ·
French or English mustard

Cut the meat into 1½-inch cubes. Split the frankfurters carefully, spread with a little pâté, and sandwich together again. Quarter the tomatoes. Put the food onto 4 long or 8 smaller metal skewers. Brush with melted margarine or butter and heat under the broiler. Heat the chicken broth and flavor with a generous amount of French or English mustard. Serve as a sauce with the kebabs.

ORANGE CONDÉ

3 or 4 oranges · 1 can (16 oz.) rice pudding ·
3 tablespoons marmalade, jam or red currant jelly

Cut the peel from the oranges, slice the fruit neatly. Blend some of the fruit with the rice pudding. Spoon into 4 individual dishes. Heat the marmalade, jam or jelly. Arrange the rest of the oranges on the rice and top with the hot preserve.

CHEESE WAFERS

8 ice cream wafer biscuits ·
4 thin slices processed or Cheddar cheese ·
1 tablespoon butter or margarine

Sandwich the wafers together with the cheese slices. Put on to a cookie tray, brush with melted butter or margarine and heat for about 3 minutes only in a hot oven, 425°F.

CHICKEN BORSCH

1 can (10½ oz.) cream of chicken soup · light cream ·
1 can (8½ oz.) beets · chopped parsley

Put the chicken soup into a small pan and heat. Add a small amount of cream and the liquid drained from the can of beets. Heat thoroughly. Garnish soup with chopped parsley.

SARDINES NIÇOISE

1 can (8¼ oz.) tomatoes · seasoning ·
1 medium-sized can sardines · 4 slices of bread ·
butter · anchovy fillets · olives

Turn the tomatoes into a pan, add seasoning and simmer until a *thick* pulp. Mash the sardines, season lightly. Toast the bread. Butter, then spread with the sardines. Heat under the broiler for a few minutes. Top with the tomato pulp, anchovy fillets and olives.

CELERY CHEESE BISCUITS
These are useful to make ahead and have on hand.

Cream 6 tablespoons butter, 1 teaspoon celery salt, a shake of pepper, ¼ cup grated Parmesan cheese and ¾ cup self-rising flour. Form into 12–15 balls and put on 2 greased and floured cookie trays. Bake for 15 minutes in the center of a very moderate oven 325–350°F. Cool on trays.

Chicken Borsch, Sardines Niçoise,
Cheese, Fresh Fruit

Queensland Cocktail

curry powder if wished (the soup already has a curry taste), the chutney, raisins, coconut and well-drained mixed vegetables. Crack the hard-cooked eggs, remove the shells. Put the eggs into a heated dish, pour over the curried mixture. Serve with bread and butter, creamed dehydrated potatoes or long grain rice. To make the curry more interesting, serve chutney, nuts, sliced bananas and/or orange in individual dishes.

To vary: It is possible to buy canned curry sauce; use this instead of the soup.

Use chicken soup instead of mulligatawny.

Use flaked canned tuna instead of eggs.

Use frozen mixed vegetables and simmer in the soup until tender.

Use dehydrated vegetables and cook as the directions on the packet, then add to the soup.

MOCK SAVARIN

1 can (16 oz.) fruit★ · 2½ tablespoons rum · small plain sponge cake

★preferably apricots, peaches or pineapple or a mixture of these fruits

Open the can of fruit, pour ½ cup of the syrup into a saucepan. Add the rum and heat. Put the cake on a dish, spoon the syrup over this. Top with the canned fruit.

To vary: Use fresh instead of canned fruit and make the syrup with ½ cup water and ¼ cup sugar. Honey or corn syrup could be used instead of sugar. Add the rum as above. Add a few drops of rum extract in place of rum. Use slices of left-over plain sponge or fruit cake. Use a liqueur, i.e. Cointreau or Curaçao, in place of the rum.

```
┌─────────────────────────────┐
│          MENU               │
│                             │
│   QUEENSLAND COCKTAIL       │
│  CURRIED HARD-COOKED EGGS   │
│    WITH MIXED VEGETABLES    │
│       MOCK SAVARIN          │
└─────────────────────────────┘
```

QUEENSLAND COCKTAIL

1 large or 2 small avocados · mayonnaise · 1 can (2¾ oz.) crabmeat · 1 green pepper · lettuce · 1 lemon

Halve the avocados, pit, remove the skin and dice the flesh. Toss with mayonnaise immediately so the avocado does not discolor. Mix with the crabmeat and diced green pepper. Shred part of a lettuce finely, put at the bottom of 4 glasses. Top with the avocado mixture. Quarter the lemon and put a section on top of each glass. Serve with a teaspoon.

To vary: Use fresh crab or other cooked shell fish.

CURRIED HARD-COOKED EGGS

4–8 eggs★ · 1 fairly large can mulligatawny soup · little curry powder (optional) · 1–2 teaspoons chutney · 1 tablespoon raisins · 1 tablespoon flaked coconut · 1 large can mixed vegetables

★depending upon your appetite

Hard-cook the eggs. Meanwhile, heat the soup, add a little

Cutlets Indienne with Sauté Potatoes

MENU

CREAM OF WATERCRESS SOUP
CUTLETS INDIENNE WITH
SAUTÉ POTATOES AND TOMATOES
CARDINAL PEACHES

CREAM OF WATERCRESS SOUP

¼ cup margarine · ½ cup flour · 1¼ cups milk ·
1¼ cups chicken stock or water and 1 chicken bouillon
cube · 1 lemon · 1 large bunch watercress ·
10 tablespoons light cream · seasoning

Make a sauce with the margarine, flour, milk and stock or
water and bouillon cube (see page 15). Add the finely grated
rind of the lemon and the stalks of the watercress (tied
together with thread) if you like a fairly hot flavor. Simmer
for 5–6 minutes, then remove the watercress stalks. Add a
little lemon juice, the cream and the finely chopped watercress
leaves. Season well and heat gently.

CUTLETS INDIENNE

2 tablespoons margarine ·
1–2 teaspoons curry powder · shake cayenne pepper ·
8 lamb cutlets · Garnish: watercress or parsley

Melt the margarine, add the curry powder and pepper.
Brush the cutlets with the mixture and broil as usual. Garnish
with watercress or parsley.

CARDINAL PEACHES

2 tablespoons red currant jelly · 2 tablespoons sugar ·
1¼ cups water · 4 firm, but ripe, peaches, skinned ·

Heat the jelly, sugar and water in a large shallow pan until jelly
melts. Add halved peaches and simmer gently for 5 minutes.

MENU

TONGUE PÂTÉ
CHICKEN BASQUE WITH
FRIED POTATOES AND BROCCOLI
CHEESE AND CRACKERS

TONGUE PÂTÉ

6 tablespoons butter · 1 clove garlic ·
1–2½ tablespoons brandy ·
1½ cups chopped cooked tongue · seasoning

Cream the butter and crushed garlic. Blend in the brandy,
then the finely chopped tongue and seasoning.

CHICKEN BASQUE

1 lb. tomatoes, skinned · 1 onion · ½ cup stock ·
¼ cup fat · 4 chicken legs and thighs ·
2½ tablespoons chopped parsley

Chop the tomatoes and onion and simmer with the stock.
Meanwhile, heat the fat and fry the chicken until just golden.
Simmer together for 15 minutes. Top with parsley.

Meanwhile, make a white sauce by the speedy method, i.e. blend the flour with the milk. Tip into a pan with the margarine or butter and stir until thickened. Season well, add the grated cheese and heat gently until melted. Put the meat and vegetables into a heated shallow casserole. Top with the sauce and a little grated nutmeg and serve at once. Serve with a green vegetable.

To vary: Add a finely sliced or diced eggplant to the potatoes and onions in the pan. You will need a little more margarine.

CORN SCRAMBLE

2 tablespoons butter or margarine ·
2 tablespoons light cream ·
1 can (8½ oz.) kernel corn · 4 eggs · seasoning

Heat the margarine in a pan with the cream. Add the drained corn and heat. Beat the eggs with seasoning. Add to the pan and scramble lightly. Serve with rolls.

SPEEDY GRILL

4 frankfurters ·
1 can (12 oz.) corned beef, sliced ·
2 tablespoons melted butter or margarine ·
canned mushrooms or tomatoes

Brush the frankfurters and sliced meat with melted butter. Cook under a hot broiler for a few minutes. Serve with canned heated mushrooms or tomatoes.

To vary: Buy fresh sausages or bacon and combine these ingredients with sliced canned ham, or buy frozen hamburgers, which cook very quickly.

CORNFLAKE FLAN

¼ cup butter or margarine · ¼ cup sugar ·
2 teaspoons corn syrup ·
1 cup cornflakes, slightly crushed · canned fruit ·
cream (optional)

Cream the butter or margarine, sugar and golden syrup. Add the cornflakes. Form into a flan shape. Either set in a cool place for a short time or brown for 10 minutes in a very moderate oven, 325°F. Fill with fruit and decorate with cream if liked.

SPEEDY MOUSSAKA

2–3 potatoes · 2–3 onions · 6 tablespoons margarine ·
1 can roast beef or Salisbury steak · ¼ cup flour ·
1¼ cups milk · 2 tablespoons margarine or butter ·
seasoning · ½ cup grated Cheddar cheese ·
grated nutmeg

Peel and grate the potatoes and onions. Heat the margarine in a pan. Cook the potatoes and onions *steadily* until just tender, about 8 minutes. Tip the roast beef or Salisbury steak into the pan and blend with the vegetables. Heat thoroughly.

COCONUT GÂTEAU

¼ cup butter · ½ cup brown sugar ·
finely grated rind and juice 1 lemon ·
2½–4 tablespoons flaked coconut · 7-inch sponge cake ·
little jam

Cream the butter and brown sugar with the lemon rind and juice. Add the coconut. Split the sponge cake across the center. If not spread with jam, cover the bottom half with a little jam then half the coconut mixture. Put the two halves together again. Spread the top of the sponge with the rest of the coconut mixture and brown under the broiler. Serve warm or cold with a jam sauce, made by heating a little jam.

MUSHROOMS À LA GRECQUE

1 tablespoon oil · juice 1 lemon · seasoning ·
½ cup white wine · ½ lb. mushrooms, cleaned

Put all the ingredients into a pan. Let them stand for about an hour if possible, although you can cook the dish immediately. Simmer gently for 10 minutes. Serve with fresh rolls and butter.

LIVER, SWEET AND SOUR

1 lb. lamb's liver · ¼ cup butter · ½ cup stock ·
1–2½ tablespoons chutney · ¼ cup raisins ·
½ tablespoon vinegar · seasoning

Cut the liver into narrow strips. Fry in the hot butter for 3 minutes only, then add the rest of the ingredients and simmer gently for 6–8 minutes.

ORANGE PANCAKES

pancake batter made with 1 cup flour, etc.
(see page 16) · 3 oranges · fat for frying · little sugar

Make the pancake batter as the recipe on page 16, but add the very finely grated rind of the 3 oranges. Cook the pancakes in the hot fat, then fill with sliced oranges. Roll up, dust with sugar and decorate with orange slices then serve.

Mushrooms à la Grecque, Liver, Sweet and Sour, with Rice and Peas, Orange Pancakes

SALMON À LA KING

1 green pepper · 1 small onion, chopped ·
¼ cup butter · ½ cup flour · 1¾ cups milk ·
1 can (8 oz.) kernel corn · 1 lemon ·
1 can (1 lb.) pink salmon · 4 slices bread

Dice the flesh of the pepper, discarding the core and seeds. Simmer for 5 minutes in water, drain. Toss the onion in the hot butter for 5 minutes, stir in the flour then blend in the milk. Bring to the boil, and stir until thickened. Add the kernel corn and liquid from the can. Add the finely grated lemon rind and juice from half the lemon, the flaked salmon and any liquid from the can (remove any skin and bones). Heat without boiling. Garnish with crisp toast and lemon.

APRICOT OMELET

6 eggs · 3 tablespoons sieved confectioners' sugar ·
2½ tablespoons light cream · ¼ cup butter ·
1 can (8½ oz.) apricots

Separate the egg yolks and the whites. Beat the yolks with 1 tablespoon sugar and the cream. Fold in the stiffly beaten egg whites. Heat the butter in a good-sized omelet pan and pour in the mixture. Allow to set for 2 minutes, move the pan under the broiler with the heat turned to medium and continue cooking until just firm. Meanwhile, heat the apricots. Cover the omelet with half the apricots, fold and tip on to a hot dish. Top with the rest of the sugar. Mark lines on top with a heated skewer (this makes a caramel effect). Serve with the rest of the apricots plus a little syrup.

MENU

PAPRIKA MUSHROOMS
CHICKEN FRICASSÉE
WITH CRUMBED POTATOES
AND GARLIC BEANS
COFFEE PEAR ALASKA

PAPRIKA MUSHROOMS

½ cup heavy cream · 1–2 teaspoons paprika ·
few drops vinegar · seasoning ·
1 can (6 oz.) button mushrooms · toast or fried bread ·
Garnish: chopped parsley

Blend the cream, paprika and vinegar. Season well. Heat the mushrooms, drain, put on rounds of toast or fried bread. Heat the cream mixture for 1–2 minutes only. Spoon over the mushrooms and top with parsley.

CHICKEN FRICASSÉE

1 cooked chicken · 1 can (10¾ oz.) asparagus soup ·
1 chicken bouillon cube · ½ cup boiling water ·
Garnish: triangles of toast, watercress

Paprika Mushrooms, Chicken Fricassée with Crumbed Potatoes and Garlic Beans, Coffee Pear Alaska

Cut the chicken into neat pieces. Remove the skin if wished. Pour the soup into a large pan. Blend the bouillon cube with the boiling water. Add to the soup, stir over a gentle heat until a smooth, fairly thin mixture. Put in the chicken pieces. Heat gently, without covering the pan, for 10 minutes. The sauce should then be the right consistency. Garnish with toast and watercress.

CRUMBED POTATOES

1 can (1 lb.) new potatoes · ¼ cup butter or margarine · 2½–4 tablespoons dry breadcrumbs

Heat the potatoes in a pan. Drain thoroughly. Melt the butter or margarine in the pan, add the breadcrumbs. Put in the potatoes and turn until coated.

GARLIC BEANS

1 lb. canned or frozen green beans · 2 tablespoons butter or margarine · 1 clove garlic, crushed

Heat or cook the beans. Drain well. Heat the butter or margarine in the pan. Add the crushed garlic. Put in the beans and blend well.

COFFEE PEAR ALASKA

1 block very firm coffee ice cream · 2 or 3 pears · 4 or 5 egg whites · ½–¾ cup sugar

Put the ice cream on an oven-proof serving dish or plate. Peel, core and quarter the pears, arrange round the ice cream. Beat the egg whites until *very stiff*. Gradually beat in half the sugar, then gently fold in the rest. Pile or pipe over the ice cream and fruit. Brown for 3–5 minutes in a very hot oven, 475°F. This dessert can be 'kept waiting' after cooking for 15–20 minutes without spoiling.

CORNED BEEF PATTIES

1½ lb. cooked potatoes · 6 tablespoons margarine · ¾ lb. corned beef · 1 tablespoon grated onion · 1 egg · seasoning ·
Coating: 1 egg · ½ cup dry breadcrumbs ·
Herbed Potatoes: 4–5 tablespoons milk ·
1 tablespoon mixed chopped fresh herbs

Mash the potatoes. Add 2 tablespoons of the margarine. Take out about half of the potatoes, mix with the flaked corned beef, onion, egg and seasoning. Form into 8 flat cakes, coat with beaten egg and dry breadcrumbs and fry in the remaining 4 tablespoons margarine until crisp and brown. Drain on absorbent paper. Meanwhile, blend the milk and herbs with the remaining potatoes. Arrange the patties on a hot dish in a border of the herbed potatoes. Serve with fried tomatoes.

Cold Weather Menus

*Once it was felt that the ideal fare for a winter's day was to start with a large
filling breakfast and to have a really 'warming' main mid-day meal: perhaps soup,
followed by a plate piled high with meat in some form, plenty of potatoes and other
vegetables, and to end the meal with a good old fashioned pudding and cheese.
This would probably be repeated with a similar type of menu in the evening. All
this may sound sensible and wise for 'keeping out the cold', but it is not the perfect
choice for wintry months. The menus in this chapter show the sort of foods you
should eat in the winter.*
All menus in this chapter serve 4 unless stated otherwise.

MENU

SPEEDY BORSCH
SWEET AND SOUR HAM WITH
CRISP TOPPED NOODLES
GREEN BEANS AND TOMATOES
CHERRY GRAPEFRUIT ALASKA

---

*This very satisfying meal can be prepared and cooked within a
very short period.*

SPEEDY BORSCH

1 medium-sized onion · 2 tablespoons fat ·
3¾ cups canned or home-made consommé or beef
stock · seasoning, including garlic salt ·
1 large cooked beet ·
Topping: little yogurt or sour cream ·
chopped parsley

Peel and grate or chop the onion and toss it in the fat until
softened but not brown. Add the consommé or beef stock
and heat thoroughly. Season well. Cut the beet into thin
strips or grate, add to the soup and warm through. Spoon
into individual soup bowls, top with yogurt or cream and
chopped parsley.

SWEET AND SOUR HAM

3 tablespoons butter or margarine ·
2 tablespoons brown sugar · 3¾ tablespoons vinegar ·
3¾ tablespoons red currant or apple jelly ·
1–2 teaspoons prepared mustard · good shake pepper ·
4 slices cooked ham, about ¼–½-inch thick

Put the butter or margarine, brown sugar, vinegar and red
currant or apple jelly into a pan, stir over a gentle heat until
the mixture forms a smooth sauce. Add the mustard and
pepper; a little salt can be added if the ham is mild in flavor.
Put in the slices of ham and heat gently.
To vary: Add a few drops of Worcestershire sauce or
Tabasco sauce.

CRISP TOPPED NOODLES

½ lb. noodles · salt ·
2 tablespoons butter or margarine ·
½ cup dry breadcrumbs · ½ cup grated cheese

Cook the noodles in boiling salted water, drain. Toss in the
butter or margarine and put in a heat-proof dish. Top with
the breadcrumbs and cheese. Brown for a few minutes only
in the oven or under the broiler. Serve the slices of ham on
this and spoon the sauce over the top.
To vary: Use spaghetti, macaroni or pasta shapes instead of
noodles.

GREEN BEANS AND TOMATOES

1 lb. frozen, fresh or canned green beans ·
3–4 tomatoes · seasoning

Cook frozen or fresh green beans or heat canned beans.
Drain, put into a pan with the peeled, thickly sliced tomatoes
and seasoning. Heat for a few minutes only and serve.
To vary: Add a chopped onion to the pan and fry for 5
minutes in 2 tablespoons butter or margarine, then add the
tomatoes and beans.
Add chopped herbs, parsley, thyme or chives to the pan
with the tomatoes.

CHERRY GRAPEFRUIT ALASKA

2 good-sized grapefruit · 1 can (8 oz.) black cherries ·
sugar to taste · ice cream · 3 egg whites · ½ cup sugar

Halve the grapefruit, remove the segments of fruit. Discard
the pith, skin and pips. Put the grapefruit pieces back into
the cases, together with some of the cherries. Sweeten to
taste. Put a spoonful of ice cream over the fruit. Beat the egg
whites until very stiff then gradually beat in sugar. Pile over
the ice cream and fruit and decorate with a few well drained
cherries. Heat for 4–5 minutes in a very hot oven, 450°F, just
until browned.
To vary: Use halved and de-seeded grapes in place of the
cherries.

*Speedy Borsch, Sweet and Sour Ham with Crisp Topped
Noodles and Green Beans and Tomatoes, Cherry Grapefruit
Alaska*

MENU

CRAB AND EGG TARTLETS
LIVER SOUFFLÉ WITH GREEN SALAD
APPLE PAN DOWDY

CRAB AND EGG TARTLETS

short crust pastry made with 1 cup flour, etc.
(see page 71) · 2 tablespoons butter · seasoning ·
3 eggs · 1 small can crabmeat ·
Garnish: watercress or parsley

Make the pastry, roll out very thinly and line 8 small patty
tins. Bake 'blind' in a hot oven, 425°F, until crisp and golden
brown. Arrange on a dish and keep warm. Heat the butter
and scramble the well-seasoned eggs blended with the flaked
crabmeat. When lightly set, pile into pastry cases. Garnish
with watercress or parsley and serve as soon as possible.
Note: The tartlet cases can be made in advance and heated
through in a moderate oven for 5–10 minutes while the egg
mixture is being cooked.
To vary: Use any other freshly cooked or canned shell fish;
chop shrimp finely.

Apple Pan Dowdy

LIVER SOUFFLÉ

2 tablespoons butter or margarine · ¼ cup flour ·
10 tablespoons milk · ¾ lb. chopped raw lamb's or
calf's liver · seasoning · pinch sugar · 3 egg yolks ·
4 egg whites, stiffly beaten

Make a thick sauce with the butter or margarine, flour and
milk. Add the liver, season well and add the sugar. Beat in
the egg yolks then fold in the egg whites. Put into a lightly
greased 7-inch soufflé dish. Bake in the center of a moderate
oven, 350–375°F, for 35 minutes or until lightly set.

APPLE PAN DOWDY

3 good-sized cooking apples ·
1–2½ tablespoons brown sugar ·
1–2½ tablespoons corn syrup · grated nutmeg ·
ground cinnamon · 1 cup self-rising flour ·
pinch salt · ¼ cup sugar · 1 egg · 5 tablespoons milk ·
¼ cup melted butter or margarine · little sugar

Peel and slice the apples. Put into a greased 8–9-inch pie
dish with the brown sugar, syrup and a sprinkling of grated
nutmeg and ground cinnamon. Do not add any water. Cover
the dish with foil and bake in the center of a moderate oven,
350°F, for about 15–20 minutes until the apples are nearly
soft. Meanwhile, make a thick batter mixture by blending the
flour, salt, sugar, egg, milk and melted butter or margarine.

Spoon the mixture over the apples, sprinkle lightly with sugar and bake in the center of a moderate oven for 30–35 minutes. Turn the pudding upside-down on to a dish. Serve with cream or brandy butter.

MENU

SPICED ORANGE JUICE
BEEF GOULASH WITH RED CABBAGE
CHEESE AND CRACKERS WITH
CELERY AND/OR CHICORY

SPICED ORANGE JUICE

2½ cups fresh or frozen orange juice ·
4 cinnamon sticks · grated nutmeg

This is not only refreshing, but as warming as hot soup. Heat the orange juice and as it heats infuse a stick of cinnamon in it. Pour into hot glasses, top with grated nutmeg and put a cinnamon stick into each glass if wished.

BEEF GOULASH

1¼ lb. chuck beef · 2–3 onions ·
¼ cup butter or margarine · 1¼ cups stock ·
2–3 teaspoons paprika ·
1 lb. peeled chopped tomatoes · seasoning ·
1 lb. potatoes (optional) ·
Garnish: yogurt (optional) · chopped parsley

Dice the meat, peel and slice the onions and toss the meat and onions in the hot butter or margarine. Blend the stock and paprika, add to the pan with the tomatoes and seasoning. Simmer gently for 1¾ hours, then add the potatoes, if using, and cook for 45 minutes. Serve with yogurt and parsley.

RED CABBAGE

1 small red cabbage · salt · 1 tablespoon butter ·
few caraway seeds (optional)

Shred the cabbage and cook in salted water, drain, add the butter. Flavor with caraway seeds, if wished.

CHEESE BOARD

Select a good variety of cheeses, i.e. a hard cheese, such as Cheddar or Cheshire, a soft cheese with 'bite', like Camembert or Brie, a delicate cheese, Bel Paese, for example, or a flavored cream cheese.

Spiced Orange Juice, Beef Goulash with Red Cabbage, Cheese and Crackers

LEMON TOMATO COCKTAIL

This makes a good warming start to the meal without being too filling.

Heat 1 pint tomato juice with the juice of 1 lemon, a shake of pepper, a pinch of grated nutmeg and a shake of celery salt.

Mexican Macaroni

MEXICAN MACARONI

Cheese sauce: 2 tablespoons margarine · ¼ cup flour · 1¼ cups milk · 1 cup grated cheese · seasoning · pinch cayenne pepper · (or use a package of cheese sauce mix with 1¼ cups milk) · ¼ lb. macaroni · 1–2 teaspoons prepared mustard · 8 frankfurters · 1 cup cooked frozen, fresh or canned peas

Make the sauce with the margarine, flour and milk. When thickened add the cheese and seasoning together with the cayenne pepper. Do not *boil* after adding the cheese, otherwise the sauce will curdle. Alternatively, make up the cheese sauce following the instructions on the package. Meanwhile, boil the macaroni in salted water, drain then add to the cheese sauce with enough mustard to give a fairly hot flavor. Chop the frankfurters add to the sauce with well-drained peas. Heat gently, then serve.

COMPÔTE OF FRUIT

½ cup water · ¼ cup sugar · about 1 lb. fresh fruit

Put the water and sugar into a saucepan, stir until the sugar has dissolved, then add the prepared fruit and simmer gently until the fruit is tender.

CHEESE STUFFED MUSHROOMS

16 large mushrooms · 2 egg yolks · 3¾ tablespoons fresh breadcrumbs · 3¾ tablespoons grated Gruyère or Cheddar cheese · seasoning · little cooked ham (optional) · To coat: 1 egg yolk · ½ cup dry breadcrumbs · fat for frying

Remove the mushroom stalks, wash and chop. Skin the mushroom caps, wash and dry. Blend the egg yolks with the breadcrumbs, cheese and seasoning. Add the mushroom stalks to this mixture and small strips of cooked ham can also be included. Spread over 8 mushrooms, then cover with the rest of the mushrooms. Dip in the egg yolk (beaten lightly and blended with a little water), coat with the dry breadcrumbs, then fry in hot shallow fat until brown on one side, turn and brown on the second side. If lightly cooked these may be warmed gently in the oven or kept hot for a short time.

CHICKEN HOT-POT

1 lb. potatoes · ¾ lb. onions · 3 tomatoes · seasoning · 4 chicken joints · about ½ cup stock · chopped fresh or dried rosemary · margarine

Put a layer of peeled thinly sliced potatoes into a casserole, cover with a layer of very thinly sliced onions and thickly sliced peeled tomatoes. Season each layer well. Put the chicken joints over the vegetables, add well-seasoned stock, a light sprinkling of rosemary, then a layer of tomatoes, onions, and a topping of potato slices. Season well, put small pieces of margarine over the potatoes. Cover the casserole and cook near the center of a very moderate oven, 325–350°F, for approximately 1¼–1½ hours. Remove the lid for the last last 20–30 minutes if wished, to brown the potatoes.

CARAMEL TOPPED RICE PUDDING

2½ tablespoons round grain rice · 1–2½ tablespoons sugar · 2½ cups milk · Topping: brown sugar

Put the rice into an oven-proof dish. Add the sugar and milk. Bake in a moderate oven, 350°F, for about 1 hour. Remove the dish from the oven, top with a layer of brown sugar and return to the oven for about 20–25 minutes, turning the heat to low, to allow the topping to caramelize.

GINGER PEARS

4 firm pears · 2 cups ginger ale or ginger beer

Peel and halve the pears. Put into a casserole and cover with ginger ale or ginger beer. Put a lid on the casserole and bake in a moderate oven, 350°F, for about 1 hour.

Chicken Hot-Pot

EGGPLANT NIÇOISE

2 medium-sized eggplants · seasoning ·
1–2 cloves garlic · 1 large onion · 1 tablespoon oil ·
2 tablespoons butter · 4–5 large tomatoes ·
Topping: chopped parsley

Wash and dry the eggplants, slice thinly, but do not peel. Sprinkle lightly with salt and leave for about 15–20 minutes; this minimizes the slightly bitter taste of the vegetable. Crush the garlic, chop the onion. Heat the oil and butter in a pan. Fry the garlic and onion gently for a few minutes, then add the peeled, chopped tomatoes. Simmer gently until the tomatoes become a purée. Add the eggplant slices and season well. Mix with the tomato purée, put a lid on the pan, and simmer steadily for 45–50 minutes. Serve hot topped with chopped parsley.

FISH KEBABS

1¼–1½ lb. firm-fleshed white fish, e.g. cod, fresh haddock or hake · about 24 small mushrooms ·
1 red pepper · 1 green pepper ·
½ cup butter or margarine · juice 1 large lemon ·
seasoning · few drops chili sauce ·
1 tablespoon chopped parsley · To serve: boiled rice

Cut the fish into 1½-inch cubes, remove skin or bones. Wash and dry the mushrooms, cut the red and green pepper into squares. Put the fish, mushrooms and peppers on to 4 or 5 metal skewers. Heat the butter or margarine, lemon juice, seasoning and chili sauce. Brush the fish and vegetables with some of the mixture. Broil quickly, turning several times, until cooked. Serve on boiled rice. Heat the remaining butter mixture, add the chopped parsley and spoon over the kebabs.

FRIED ZUCCHINI

1 lb. zucchini · seasoning · ¼ cup flour ·
shallow or deep fat for frying

Wash, dry and cut the zucchini into ¼–½-inch slices. Coat in well-seasoned flour, and fry until crisp and golden brown. Drain on absorbent paper before serving.

CHOCOLATE PUDDING WITH RUM SAUCE

2 squares unsweetened chocolate ·
few drops vanilla extract ·
¼ cup butter or margarine · ½ cup sugar · 2 eggs ·
1½ cups all-purpose flour and 1½ teaspoons baking powder · 7½ tablespoons milk

Eggplant Niçoise, Fish Kebabs with Rice and Fried Zucchini, Chocolate Pudding and Rum Sauce

Put the chocolate, vanilla extract and butter or margarine into a bowl, melt over a pan of hot water. Remove the bowl from the pan and cool the chocolate mixture slightly. Add the sugar and blend thoroughly. Beat in the eggs then the flour and milk. Grease and flour a 5 cup bowl, put in the mixture, cover and steam for 1 hour. Turn out and serve with rum sauce.

RUM SAUCE

2½ tablespoons cornstarch · 1¼ cups milk ·
2½ tablespoons sugar · 2 tablespoons rum

Blend the cornstarch with the milk. Put into a saucepan with the sugar and heat, stirring well, until thickened. Add rum to taste.

To vary: Use 2 tablespoons brandy in place of the rum.

MOROCCAN LAMB

8 small or 4 large lamb chops · 12 cooked prunes ·
½ cup syrup from cooking the prunes · ½ cup water ·
pinch turmeric · about 1 tablespoon sugar or honey ·
2 onions · seasoning

Put the chops and prunes into a shallow casserole. Heat the prune syrup, water, turmeric and sugar or honey with the finely chopped onions and seasoning. Pour over the lamb and prunes. If the liquid does not quite cover the meat and prunes add a little more hot water or prune juice, but do not use too much liquid. Cover the casserole and bake in the center of a very moderate over, 325°F, for 1¼ hours. Any liquid left could be served with the meat, or served Moroccan style in a separate bowl, seasoned with a little chili powder. Serve with boiled noodles tossed in butter and celery.

To vary: Use sliced oranges and ½ cup orange juice instead of the prunes and prune juice.

BRAISED CELERY

3 tablespoons fat · 1 large onion · ¼ cup flour ·
1¼ cups brown stock · 1 bunch celery · seasoning

Heat the fat and fry the chopped onion. Stir in the flour, blend in the stock. Bring to the boil, cook until thickened. Cut the well-washed and dried celery into neat portions. Blend with the sauce, season, and transfer to a deep casserole. Cover well and cook in moderate oven, 350°F, for 30 minutes. The amount of sauce in this dish is fairly small as the lamb is cooked with a sauce and you just need enough to keep the celery from becoming dry. Double the amount of fat, flour and liquid if you want a good amount of sauce to serve with meat, poultry or fish.

To vary: Fry 1 or 2 chopped slices of bacon with the onion, then flavor the sauce with a little red wine and herbs. Root vegetables such as carrots and turnips may be braised too.

TOURNEDOS BÉARNAISE ·

Sauce: 3 tablespoons white or white wine vinegar ·
3¾ tablespoons tarragon vinegar ·
1 shallot or small onion · 3 egg yolks · ½ cup butter ·
½–1 teaspoon each chopped fresh tarragon and
chervil or good pinch dried herbs · seasoning ·
4–6 fillet steaks, 1–2 inches thick · butter

Make the sauce before cooking the meat and keep it hot over
a very low heat. Put the vinegars into a pan with the peeled
shallot or onion. Simmer the vinegars until reduced to
2–2½ tablespoons, then allow to cool. Put the egg yolks and
the strained vinegars into the top of a double boiler or a
bowl over a pan of hot, but not boiling, water. Beat until
thick. While this is thickening allow the butter to soften
slightly. Gradually beat in the butter – *do this very gradually.*
Lastly add the herbs. Season well. Tie (or ask the butcher to
do this) the steaks into rounds (tournedos). Brush with butter
and follow the instructions for broiling below. Serve with the
Béarnaise Sauce, creamed potatoes and cauliflower.

To broil steaks: Preheat the broiler to seal the outside of
the meat as quickly as possible. Brush the meat with a
generous amount of butter (or oil). Broil quickly for approximately 2 minutes on either side. If you like rare meat,
serve at once, if not, lower the heat and cook for a further
4–6 minutes or until cooked to personal taste.

Banana and Lemon Cream

BANANA AND LEMON CREAM

1 package lemon-flavored gelatin ·
2 cups boiling water · 4 teaspoons lemon juice ·
1¼ tablespoons sugar · 1¼ cups heavy cream ·
2 egg whites · 5 small bananas · 20–24 Lady fingers ·
few glacé cherries

Dissolve the gelatin in the water. Add half the lemon juice
and all the sugar. Chill until beginning to set. To hurry
this process stand over a bowl of ice cubes. When the jelly
is firm, beat until frothy and add 1 cup cream, whipped until
it stands in peaks. Fold in the stiffly beaten egg whites and
3 sliced bananas. Spoon into a 1½ quart tin or mold (rinsed
in cold water). When set, turn out. Press cream-coated Lady
fingers around the edge and top with the remaining whipped
cream, sliced bananas (dipped in remaining lemon juice)
and cherries.

GINGER GRAPEFRUIT

2 grapefruit · ¼ cup brown sugar ·
pinch ground ginger · 2 tablespoons preserved ginger ·
2 tablespoons butter

Halve the grapefruit, remove the segments and mix with
half the sugar, the ground ginger and chopped preserved
ginger. Spoon back into grapefruit skins, spread with butter
and the rest of the sugar. Heat for 2–3 minutes only under
the broiler.

STEAK AND KIDNEY PUDDING

Filling: 1 lb. round steak ·
¾ lb. beef kidney (or 3–4 lambs' kidneys) ·
seasoning · 2 tablespoons flour · water or stock ·
Pastry: 2 cups all-purpose flour · salt ·
½ cup shredded suet or ⅔ cup 70° shortening · water

Cut the meat and kidney into neat pieces; discard any gristle
and skin. Mix with the seasoned flour. Put on one side – do
not add the water or stock yet. Sift the flour and salt. Add
the suet or shortening and water to make a soft rolling dough.
Roll out thinly and use three-quarters to line a 5 cup bowl.
Put in the meat and water or stock to half cover this. Roll
out the remaining pastry to form a lid, wet the edges and press
this on top of the pudding. Cover with greased waxed paper
and foil. Steam in a large kettle, half-filled with water, for
4–5 hours then serve. Additional gravy may be served or
fill up the pudding (after cutting the first slice) with un-
thickened brown stock. Makes 4 *large* servings.

To vary: This pudding is excellent if made with lean diced
lamb or mutton instead of beef. Add a light sprinkling of
finely chopped mint to the meat and kidney; lambs' kidneys
can be used instead of beef kidney, but these are more
expensive. Diced chicken plus diced chickens' livers is
another excellent filling.
Sliced onions, mushrooms, and mixed diced root vegetables
may also be used with the meat filling.
Older grouse or pheasant, neatly jointed, may be used in
this type of pudding.

*Ginger Grapefruit, Steak and Kidney Pudding, Brussels
Sprouts*

Slimming Menus

Do not imagine that slimming menus are necessarily monotonous and dull. Obviously, there are many high-calorie or fattening foods you must avoid but if you make slimming meals interesting and imaginative, there is a much greater chance of success. I have planned family menus for 4 people that are relatively low in calories and added hints for the 'non-slimmers' as well.

MENU

**HARLEQUIN SOUFFLÉ OMELET
WITH BROCCOLI
HOT MELON WITH GINGER**

HARLEQUIN SOUFFLÉ OMELET

6–8 eggs · 1 cup cottage cheese · seasoning ·
1 tablespoon chopped parsley ·
1–2½ tablespoons chopped chives or scallions ·
¼ cup butter* ·
Topping: slices of red pepper or tomato and green pepper
If butter is not allowed on your particular diet, you must cook the omelet in a 'non-stick' pan. Heat the pan, without any fat, then add the egg mixture.

Separate the egg whites from the yolks. Beat the yolks with the cottage cheese and seasoning until a smooth well blended mixture. Add the chopped parsley and chopped chives or scallions. Next fold in the stiffly beaten egg whites. Heat the butter in a very large pan. Pour in the egg mixture. Cook steadily for about 5–6 minutes, then put the pan under a medium broiler and cook for a further 3–4 minutes until set. Slip out of the pan (do not try to fold) on to a hot dish. Top with slices of red pepper, or tomato and green pepper. Serve at once.
For non-slimmers: Add toast, bread or rolls to the meal and top the broccoli with plenty of butter.

HOT MELON WITH GINGER

1 ripe melon · 6 tablespoons fresh orange juice ·
ground ginger

Slice the melon in wedges and remove the seeds. Moisten with the orange juice, sprinkle with a little ground ginger and warm in a moderate oven, 350°F, for about 20 minutes or until piping hot.
For non-slimmers: Blend a little preserved ginger syrup with the orange juice and top with pieces of preserved ginger. Omit the ground ginger if wished.

MENU

**FISH IN WINE SAUCE WITH
BAKED STUFFED MUSHROOMS
CHEESE AND STARCH-REDUCED ROLL**

FISH IN WINE SAUCE
Fish is a low-calorie, high-protein food, so is ideal for slimmers.

Fillets of whiting, plaice, sole or other white fish ·
seasoning · dry white wine ·
few halved de-seeded grapes ·
little diced green and red pepper ·

Season and fold the fish fillets. Put into a shallow oven-proof dish. Cover with wine, add the grapes and diced peppers and cover the dish. Bake for 20–30 minutes (according to the size of the fillets) in the center of a moderate oven, 375°F.

BAKED STUFFED MUSHROOMS

¾ lb. fairly large mushrooms · 2–3 large tomatoes ·
1 small onion · 2 tablespoons butter or margarine ·
1 tablespoon chopped parsley · seasoning

Wash the mushrooms and remove the stalks. Chop these and blend with the skinned chopped tomatoes, grated onion, butter or margarine, parsley and seasoning. Put the mushrooms on a large greased oven-proof dish. Top with the stuffing. Cover with foil and cook in the oven for the same length of time as the fish. Serve hot.
For non-slimmers: Top the mushrooms with a little butter or margarine and serve another cooked vegetable with the meal.
To vary: Add a little finely chopped, lean ham to the stuffing. Add a little prepared mustard or Worcestershire sauce to the stuffing.

Harlequin Soufflé Omelet with Broccoli, Hot Melon with Ginger

SHRIMP IN ASPIC

⅓ lb. cooked, de-veined shrimp ·
1 envelope unflavored gelatin · 2 cups water ·
2 chicken bouillon cubes ·
1½ tablespoons tomato paste ·
few drops Worcestershire sauce

If shrimp are large, cut into pieces and place in 4 small molds or dishes. Soften the gelatin in ½ cup water. Combine 1½ cups water and bouillon cubes and heat until bouillon cubes are dissolved. Add softened gelatin and stir until gelatin is dissolved. Cool. Stir in tomato paste and Worcestershire sauce. Pour over top of shrimp. Chill until set.
For non-slimmers: Top with a spoonful of mayonnaise.

STUFFED STEAKS

4 fairly thick fillet or club steaks · 2 lambs' kidneys ·
seasoning · chopped parsley ·
2 peeled, chopped tomatoes · melted fat

Stuffed Steaks

Cut horizontally across three-quarters of each steak to make a pocket. Chop the kidneys finely, season well and add the parsley and tomatoes. Insert the stuffing into the steaks and broil until cooked to personal taste. Use the minimum amount of melted fat to baste the meat. If preferred, wrap each steak in a square of foil and bake for 20–35 minutes (depending upon how you like the meat cooked) in a hot oven, 425°F; 20 minutes will give a very rare steak.
For non-slimmers: Blend a little chopped bacon or 2 tablespoons butter with the kidney filling. Purée or chop the spinach and blend with a little heavy cream. Season well.
To vary: Use lamb's or calf's liver is place of kidney in the stuffing. Use fillet of veal in place of steak. Roll up and secure with wooden skewers or fine string. Bake in foil in a hot oven for about 35–45 minutes.

JUNKET

2½ cups skimmed milk · little sugar substitute ·
2½ teaspoons rennet · grated nutmeg ·
Topping: fresh fruit

Heat the skimmed milk to blood heat. Add a little sugar substitute. Add the rennet (this amount is necessary with pasteurized milk). Pour into 4 dishes, top with grated nutmeg and allow to clot at room temperature. Top with a few slices of any fresh unsweetened fruit (oranges are particularly good but avoid banana) just before serving.
For non-slimmers: Spoon lightly whipped cream (sweetened to taste) on the junket then add the fruit.

Watercress Eggs

MENU

WATERCRESS EGGS
DEVILED WHITE FISH
WITH GRILLED TOMATOES
AND SPINACH
YOGURT AND ORANGE SUNDAE

WATERCRESS EGGS

4 eggs · seasoning · squeeze lemon juice ·
2½ tablespoons skimmed milk ·
3½–5 tablespoons chopped watercress leaves · lettuce

Hard-cook the eggs and halve lengthways. Remove the yolks, mash with seasoning. Add the lemon juice, skimmed milk (to give a soft consistency) and the chopped watercress leaves. Press into the white halves and serve on a bed of lettuce.
Note: If you are being extra careful with calories, have half an egg only as an hors d'oeuvre.
For non-slimmers: Top each portion with mayonnaise.
To vary: Use chopped canned asparagus tips in place of watercress.

DEVILED WHITE FISH

1–2 teaspoons Worcestershire sauce ·
½ teaspoon curry powder · pinch cayenne pepper ·
¼–½ teaspoon celery salt ·
2 tablespoons butter, melted · 4 portions white fish

Blend the Worcestershire sauce, curry powder, cayenne pepper and celery salt with the melted butter. Brush over the fish portions and cook under a hot broiler. Serve with grilled tomatoes and cooked spinach. Do not cream the spinach or add any butter. Instead season well and add a little grated nutmeg.
For non-slimmers: Top the broiled fish with a generous portion of extra flavored butter.
To vary: Use lemon butter, parsley butter, tomato butter or anchovy butter.

YOGURT AND ORANGE SUNDAE

6 oranges · plain yogurt

Cut the peel from the oranges and then cut the fruit into rings or segments. Divide between 4 glasses and top with plain yogurt.
For non-slimmers: Add a generous portion of sweetened whipped cream or sweeten the orange slices (honey or brown sugar is delicious).

MENU

**CLEAR TOMATO SOUP
CITRUS LAMB CHOPS
WITH GREEN SALAD
FROSTED APPLE**

CLEAR TOMATO SOUP

2½ cups canned tomato juice · 2–3 sticks celery ·
6–8 scallions · sprig parsley · seasoning ·
½ cup yogurt (optional)

Heat the tomato juice, add the finely chopped celery, scallions, parsley and seasoning. The soup can be topped with a spoonful of yogurt if wished.

For non-slimmers: Top each portion with a little sour cream or a spoonful of heavy fresh cream.

To vary: This is delicious as an ice-cold soup for hot weather.

CITRUS LAMB CHOPS

lamb chops · oranges

Bake or broil lamb chops – do not fry. Add slices of orange to the broiler or roasting pan a few minutes before the meat is cooked.

For non-slimmers: Serve with baked, creamed or new potatoes.

GREEN SALAD

Eat plenty of green salads when on a slimming diet – they are low in calories and give you valuable vitamins and minerals. Choose the low-calorie salad ingredients, i.e. lettuce, endive, chicory, cucumber and green or red pepper.

Shred or chop and arrange a generous portion of salad in bowls or on plates. To make a low-calorie dressing, blend plain yogurt with plenty of seasoning and a squeeze of lemon juice.

FROSTED APPLE

1 lb. apples · sugar substitute · 2 eggs

Cook the peeled and cored apples until a smooth thick purée. Add a little sugar substitute to sweeten. Allow to cool. Separate the egg yolks from the whites. Blend the yolks with the apple, then fold in the stiffly beaten whites. Freeze lightly.

For non-slimmers: Top each portion with cream or vanilla ice cream and chopped nuts or grated or flaked coconut.

Clear Tomato Soup, Citrus Lamb Chops with Green Salad

Light Meal Menus

There are a number of occasions when a light menu is required. Many people dislike a heavy lunch, particularly when working hard. A light meal is ideal for a late supper or when one is over-tired or has some digestive disorder. If light meals are chosen for medical reasons, avoid highly spiced or exotic dishes containing rich sauces. There are many interesting dishes based on milk, eggs and fish which are easily digested.

All menus in this chapter serve 4 unless stated otherwise.

MENU

OMELET ESPAGNOLE
WITH BROCCOLI
COTTAGE CHEESE AND
APPLE RINGS WITH
CRACKERS AND BUTTER

MENU

WALDORF SALAD
CURRIED SEA-FOOD SCALLOPS
CHEESE AND CRACKERS

OMELET ESPAGNOLE

This has almost exactly the same kind of ingredients as the usual Tortilla (Spanish Omelet) but the omelet is a soufflé type.

1 onion · 2–3 peeled tomatoes · 1 green pepper · a few mushrooms · a little oil · 2½–4 tablespoons stock · seasoning · strips cooked ham or sausage (optional) · diced cooked potato and any other cooked vegetables, e.g. peas, carrots, onions · ¼ cup butter · 5–6 eggs · 2½ tablespoons milk

Chop the onion, tomatoes, green pepper and mushrooms and sauté in the oil for a few minutes. Add the stock so the mixture is kept hot and moist. Season well and put in strips of cooked ham or sausage if wished, together with the diced cooked potato and any other vegetables. Put the butter into a large, shallow oven-proof dish: put this into the oven to heat. Separate the egg yolks from the whites. Beat the yolks with seasoning and the milk, then fold in the stiffly beaten whites. Remove the dish from the oven and pour in the omelet mixture. Bake for about 15 minutes above the center of a hot oven, 425°F, until lightly set. Slip out of the dish if wished, top with the hot vegetable mixture and serve at once.

To vary: If preferred, cook as ordinary omelets and fill with the mixture.

COTTAGE CHEESE AND APPLE RINGS

4 dessert apples · 1 cup cottage cheese · ½ cup raisins · ¼ cup nuts

Core the apples and cut into rings, spread with the cottage cheese and top with raisins and/or nuts. Serve with cheese crackers and butter.

To vary: Use a light cream cheese.

WALDORF SALAD

This rather sweet salad is a refreshing start to a meal.

1 crisp lettuce · 2 dessert apples · few sticks celery · 4 tablespoons mayonnaise · ¼ cup chopped walnuts, cashew nuts or almonds · Garnish: few fresh or well drained canned grapefruit segments · grapes or melon balls

Put a layer of lettuce into a salad bowl. Core and dice the apples, chop the celery. Mix with the mayonnaise and pile onto the lettuce. Top with the chopped nuts. Garnish with the grapefruit segments and grapes or melon balls.

CURRIED SEA-FOOD SCALLOPS

3 tablespoons butter or margarine · 6 tablespoons flour · 1–2 teaspoons curry powder · 1¼ cups milk · seasoning · 2½–4 tablespoons light cream · about 1 lb. mixed fish★ · Topping: dry breadcrumbs · Garnish (optional): unshelled shrimp

★i.e. flaked cooked white fish, shrimp, scallops or canned or fresh crabmeat, and a little canned tuna

Make a creamy curry sauce with the butter or margarine, flour, curry powder and milk. When thickened add seasoning and cream. Blend with the mixed fish. Put into scallop shells. Top with breadcrumbs and heat under the broiler or in the oven. Garnish with shrimp if wished.

To vary: To make a more substantial dish, arrange a layer of cooked long-grain rice in a shallow, heat-proof dish. Top with the curry mixture and heat as above. The sauce may be flavored with cheese, anchovy extract or parsley instead of curry.

Waldorf Salad, Curried Sea-Food Scallops, Cheese

Mexican Frankfurters

MENU

**BOILED HAM WITH
SWEET AND SOUR ONIONS
MUSHROOM SALAD
CUCUMBER YOGURT SALAD
FRESH FRUIT**

BOILED HAM

Either serve the cooked ham cold, or heat in a little stock or water with a bouillon cube. Slice neatly.

SWEET AND SOUR ONIONS

2½ teaspoons cornstarch · ½ cup white wine vinegar ·
2½ tablespoons honey ·
2½–4 tablespoons tomato chutney ·
½ cup white stock · seasoning · 1 large cooked beet ·
about 12 pickled onions

Blend the cornstarch with the vinegar, honey, chutney, stock and seasoning. Put into a pan and cook until thickened. Add the beet, finely diced or grated, and cool. Pour over the well drained onions and leave for several hours.

MUSHROOM SALAD

¼ lb. button mushrooms · seasoning ·
4 tablespoons oil · 2 tablespoons vinegar ·
fresh herbs (optional)

Slice the well washed and dried mushrooms, toss in well seasoned oil and vinegar and top with chopped fresh herbs.

CUCUMBER YOGURT SALAD

½ cucumber · 1¼ cups plain yogurt · seasoning ·
squeeze lemon juice · shake paprika

slice the cucumber and mix with, or top with, the yogurt mixed with seasoning, lemon juice and paprika. Serve very cold.

MENU

**ORANGE JUICE
MEXICAN FRANKFURTERS
WITH GREEN SALAD
CHEESE AND CRACKERS**

MEXICAN FRANKFURTERS

3 oz. shell or other shaped macaroni · salt ·
1¼ cups consommé · few drops chili sauce ·
4 tomatoes · 6–8 frankfurters ·
Garnish: 2 pineapple rings · 1 tomato · parsley

Cook the macaroni in boiling salted water, drain and mix with the consommé, chilli sauce and sliced tomatoes and frankfurters. Heat steadily for 20 minutes. Put into a serving dish and top with pineapple rings, sliced tomato and parsley sprigs or chopped parsley.

1 small white or brown loaf of unsliced bread ·
6 tablespoons butter or margarine ·
2 packages (8 oz.) cream cheese ·
3–4 peeled tomatoes (see below) · seasoning ·
piece cucumber · ½ cup canned or cooked salmon ·
3–4 hard-cooked eggs · 4 tablespoons mayonnaise ·
1 lettuce · ½ cup salted peanuts ·
Garnish: cucumber · radishes ·
anchovy fillets

Remove the crusts from the loaf and cut the loaf into 4 slices lengthways. Spread each slice with butter or margarine.
Layer 1 Put the first slice of bread on a board, buttered side up, and spread with some of the cream cheese and sliced tomato.
Layer 2 Top with the second slice, buttered side up, and cover with well-seasoned sliced cucumber and flaked salmon.
Layer 3 Put the third slice of bread on this and cover with chopped hard-cooked eggs blended with mayonnaise and finely shredded lettuce. Cover with the last slice of bread, buttered side downwards. Coat the top and sides of the sandwich with cream cheese and press salted nuts against the sides. Lift on to a bed of green salad and garnish the top with twists of cucumber, radishes and/or a lattice of well-drained anchovy fillets. The salad can be served separately if preferred.

To vary: Other fillings can be used in place of those given above, i.e. scrambled eggs and finely chopped green pepper, cream cheese and chopped nuts or raisins.
To peel tomatoes: Put the tomatoes into boiling water for 1 minute. Lift out, put into cold water, then remove the skin.

TOMATO SOUFFLÉS

4 very large firm tomatoes★ · seasoning ·
3 egg yolks ·
about 2 tablespoons fine fresh breadcrumbs ·
1–2 teaspoons finely chopped chives or scallion ·
2 egg whites
★or use 8 smaller tomatoes

Halve the tomatoes and scoop out the pulp carefully so the tomato cases are left intact. Season the cases. Chop the pulp very finely, add the egg yolks and breadcrumbs to make a creamy consistency. Blend with a generous amount of seasoning and the chopped chives or scallion; fold in the stiffly beaten egg whites. Spoon the mixture into the tomato cases. Stand on a flat oven-proof dish and bake for about 12 minutes in a moderately hot oven, 375–400°F, until golden brown. Serve at once.
To vary: Use grated cheese in place of breadcrumbs. Add a few chopped anchovies or a little anchovy extract to the egg yolks.
Omit the chives or scallion and use 1 teaspoon chopped thyme or sage instead.

Tomato Soufflés, Salad Sandwich Loaf, Fresh Fruit

Crab Bisque

MENU

**CRAB BISQUE
AVOCADO SALAD**
This menu serves 4–6

CRAB BISQUE

1 medium-sized cooked crab or 1 can (8 oz.)
crabmeat · 2 cups fish stock* or water · 1 lemon ·
seasoning · *bouquet garni* · 1 onion · 5 mushrooms ·
¼ cup butter · 1¼ cups light cream · 2 egg yolks ·
2½ tablespoons sherry
made by boiling fish bones or a fish head

Remove all the meat from the fresh crab and put on one side.
Put the stock or water, pared lemon rind, a little lemon juice,
seasoning and the *bouquet garni* in a pan. Add the shell if
using fresh crab. Cover the pan and simmer gently for 30
minutes. Chop the onion, slice the mushrooms and toss in
the hot butter. Add the strained stock and the flaked crabmeat
and heat gently. Blend the cream with the egg yolks, add to
the crab mixture and simmer gently just until thickened.
Add the sherry.

AVOCADO SALAD

4 tablespoons salad oil
2½ tablespoons white vinegar · seasoning ·
2 large ripe avocados · 2 oranges · 2 firm tomatoes ·
lettuce   piece cucumber

Blend the oil, vinegar and seasoning and put into a bowl.
Halve the avocados, pit and slice and put into the oil and
vinegar dressing. Cut the peel from the oranges and cut the
oranges into neat segments. Slice the tomatoes. Arrange the
avocado, orange and tomato slices on shredded lettuce,
garnish with twists of cucumber. This salad is delicious for
a light main course or to serve with meat or poultry.

MENU

**CAULIFLOWER SURPRISE WITH
CRISPBREAD AND BUTTER
APRICOT DIPLOMAT**
This menu serves 4–6

CAULIFLOWER SURPRISE

*This looks like Cauliflower Mornay (cauliflower cheese) but
underneath you have a layer of savoury vegetables that turn
this into a 'meal in a dish'.*

2–3 medium-sized onions · 2 peeled tomatoes ·
6 mushrooms · ½ cup margarine ·
1 small can sweet corn · few cooked or canned peas ·
few tablespoons diced cooked ham ·
1 medium-sized cauliflower · seasoning · ½ cup flour ·
1¾ cup milk · ½ cup grated cheese

Slice the onions, tomatoes and mushrooms and toss in half
the margarine until tender. Add the well drained corn, peas
and diced ham. Heat gently but do not over-cook and keep

46

Cauliflower Surprise

hot until required. Meanwhile, cook the cauliflower in boiling salted water until just tender. Make a white sauce with the remaining margarine, flour, milk, ½ cup water from cooking the cauliflower and seasoning. When the sauce has thickened, blend about one-quarter with the vegetable mixture and put into a hot deep serving dish or casserole. Put the cauliflower on top. Add the grated cheese to the remaining sauce and spoon over the cauliflower. Brown under the broiler and serve at once.

To vary: Fry a few slices of bacon until crisp, then crumble and sprinkle over the cauliflower.

APRICOT DIPLOMAT

1 medium-sized can halved apricots ·
1 sponge cake layer · 3 eggs · ¼ cup sugar ·
1¾ cups warm milk

Strain the syrup from the apricots and reserve 4–5 table-spoons. Put a layer of apricots at the bottom of a 1 quart greased bowl. Crumble the sponge cake and spread over the apricots. Beat the eggs and sugar, add the warm milk and reserved apricot syrup. Pour over the sponge cake. Cover the bowl with greased foil or waxed paper and steam for about 1¼ hours over hot, but not boiling, water. By this time the pudding should be nearly set. Lift off the cover and arrange the rest of the apricots over the custard mixture. Cover again and continue steaming for 15–30 minutes. Serve hot or cold but allow the pudding to stand for about 5 minutes before turning out of the bowl.

To vary: Crushed pineapple, either fresh or canned, could be used in place of apricots. An unusual and delicious variation is to substitute fresh or canned passion fruit or peaches for the apricots.

MENU

**SOLE SUPRÊME
CREAMED SPINACH
RASPBERRY APPLE SUNDAE**

SOLE SUPRÊME

8 small fillets sole · 1 cup white wine · seasoning ·
2 tablespoons butter · ¼ cup flour ·
10 tablespoons milk · 2 egg yolks ·
2½ tablespoons sherry ·
Garnish: small fried croûtons of bread

Fold the fish, put into a shallow pan, poach in the wine for 6–7 minutes, season well. Meanwhile, make a thick sauce with butter, flour and milk. Lift fish on to a hot dish, strain the liquid into the sauce. Stir well. Beat the egg yolks and sherry together and beat into the sauce. Simmer for 1–2 minutes only, taste and add extra seasoning if desired. Spoon over the fish and top with the croûtons.

To make croûtons: Dice brown or white bread into ½-inch squares. Fry in hot deep or shallow fat or oil until golden. Drain on absorbent paper.

RASPBERRY APPLE SUNDAE

Blend 2–3 diced dessert apples with a little lemon juice (peel the fruit if wished). Blend with 3–4 cartons raspberry flavored yogurt and add a few seedless raisins and chopped nuts.

Prune and Nut Coleslaw: Mix chopped nuts, shredded cabbage and a few cooked well-drained prunes together. Blend with a little mayonnaise.

Pear and Nut Salad: Mix peeled and sliced pears with some chopped nuts and mayonnaise to bind. Put on to a bed of lettuce and garnish with endive.

WELSH RAREBIT

There are many recipes for Welsh Rarebit, but this is an easy one.

⅔ lb. Cheddar cheese · 5 tablespoons butter · 5 eggs · seasoning · 2½ tablespoons beer or milk · 1 teaspoon prepared mustard · 4 slices bread

Grate the cheese and blend with half the butter, 1 egg, the seasoning, beer or milk and the mustard. Toast the bread and spread with the rest of the butter, and the cheese mixture. Toast under the broiler while poaching the remaining 4 eggs. Lift the eggs on to the cheese mixture and serve at once.
Note: If you like a stiffer topping, use the egg yolk only and 1 tablespoon beer or milk.

Welsh Rarebit

To vary: Put slices of ham on the toast and then top with the cheese and egg.

SOME NEW SALAD IDEAS

As fruit blends well with cheese, try some of these colorful looking dishes to serve with a Welsh Rarebit or with cheese.

Apple and Celery Salad: Dice the tender sticks from ½ bunch celery. Dice several dessert apples and mix with a little mayonnaise, French dressing or lemon juice. There is no need to remove the peel, as this gives color to the salad. Arrange on a bed of shredded lettuce and garnish with olives.
Pineapple and Orange Salad: Mix diced well-drained canned or fresh pineapple with orange segments. Put on to a bed of lettuce, watercress and endive and top with a little well-seasoned yogurt.

Haddock Charlotte with Creamed Carrots and Duchesse Potatoes, Peach Madrilenes

HADDOCK CHARLOTTE

4–5 large slices bread and butter · 1–1¼ lb. fresh haddock · 1 egg · ½ cup milk · seasoning · 1 teaspoon finely grated lemon rind · 1–2 teaspoons finely chopped parsley · Garnish: segments of tomato and lemon

Cut the crusts from the bread and butter. Flake or grind the fish finely. Blend with the egg, milk, seasoning, lemon rind and parsley. Cut the bread into fingers and put half at the bottom of a 1½-quart pie dish with the buttered side touching the bottom of the dish. Spoon the fish mixture over this. Top with fingers of bread and butter with the buttered sides uppermost. Bake for 45–55 minutes in the center of a very moderate to moderate oven, 325–350°F, until the bread topping is crisp. Garnish with segments of tomato and lemon.

CREAMED CARROTS

1 lb. carrots · 1 tablespoon butter or margarine · 2½–4 tablespoons light cream

Cook and mash the carrots, then blend with the butter or margarine and cream. Pile into the serving dish.

DUCHESSE POTATOES

1½ lb. potatoes · ¼ cup butter or margarine · 1 or 2 egg yolks

Cook and mash the potatoes, then purée to ensure all the lumps are removed. Beat the butter or margarine and the egg yolks into the mashed potato. Do not add milk as this makes the potato shapes spread badly. Pipe or pile into large rose or pyramid shapes on a greased oven-proof dish or cooking tray. Heat through and brown in the oven.

PEACH MADRILENES

12 grapes · 1 orange · ½ cup heavy cream · sugar · 4 large or 8 smaller peach halves

Halve and de-seed the grapes, skin if wished. Remove the skin, pith and pips from the orange and cut the fruit into neat pieces. Whip the cream until it just holds its shape. Sweeten to taste. Add the grapes and orange segments and pile into the peach halves.
To vary: Thick smooth custard, sour cream or plain yogurt may be used in place of cream.

Family Menus

The essence of most family meal planning is to create interesting meals, without being unduly extravagant, or taking too long in preparation. It is important to give the family meals that are nutritionally well balanced. All of the family need adequate amounts of protein. Fortunately, there are many ways in which we can obtain protein – from meat and poultry, fish, eggs, cheese, from the pulses (beans, peas, lentils), milk and bread.

These menus concentrate on nutritious meals that provide pleasant tasting and attractive looking dishes which do not require a great deal of time spent on them. All menus in this chapter serve 4 unless stated to the contrary.

MENU

**CHEESE PUDDING WITH
MIXED VEGETABLES
TREACLE TART**

This menu serves 4–6

CHEESE PUDDING

**1 cup fresh breadcrumbs · 1¾ cups milk ·
2 tablespoons butter or margarine ·
1½ cups grated Cheddar cheese · 3 eggs · seasoning**

Put the breadcrumbs into a bowl. Heat the milk with the butter or margarine, pour over the crumbs and leave for 10 minutes. Add the grated cheese, the well-beaten eggs and seasoning. Pour into a 1½-quart oven-proof dish and bake in the center of a moderately hot oven, 400°F, for about 30–35 minutes until well risen and golden brown.
Mixed vegetables: Cook diced mixed vegetables until tender, strain and serve with a parsley sauce or topped with tomato paste.
Planning wisely: 'Tired', rather dry pieces of cheese may be grated, stored in bags or jars in a cool place and used up in dishes, such as the cheese pudding.

TREACLE TART

**short crust pastry made with 1½ cups flour, etc.
(see page 71) · grated rind ½ lemon ·
1 tablespoon lemon juice · 5 tablespoons corn syrup ·
breadcrumbs or crushed cornflakes**

Roll out the pastry and line an 8–9-inch pie plate. Prick the pastry and bake 'blind' towards the top of a moderately hot oven, 400°F, until set. Meanwhile, mix the grated lemon rind with the lemon juice, corn syrup and enough breadcrumbs or cornflakes to give a soft consistency. Cover the pastry with this. Move to a cooler part of the oven, or lower the heat slightly, and continue cooking for a further 15–20 minutes until the pastry is crisp. Serve hot with cream, or allow to cool and serve cold.

MENU

**TIPSY CHOPS WITH SAVORY POTATO CAKE
GREEN VEGETABLES
SAUCER PANCAKES AND FRUIT**

TIPSY CHOPS

**seasoning · 4 large or 8 smaller lamb chops ·
5 tablespoons red wine, orange juice or stock**

Season the chops and put into an oven-proof dish. Spoon the the wine, orange juice or stock over them (each gives a different flavor). Cover and cook for 25–30 minutes in the center of a hot oven, 425°F.

SAVORY POTATO CAKE

**1 lb. potatoes · 2 large onions · seasoning ·
2 tablespoons melted margarine or oil**

Peel or scrape the potatoes and slice very thinly. Peel and slice the onions equally thinly. Pack a greased tin with layers of potato and onion, beginning and ending with potatoes, and season layers well. Brush the top layer with melted margarine of oil. Cover tightly. Bake in the coolest part of a hot oven, 425°F, for 1–1¼ hours. Turn out like a cake.

SAUCER PANCAKES

**¼ cup butter · ¼ cup sugar · 2 eggs ·
1 cup all-purpose flour · pinch salt ·
10 tablespoons milk ·
Filling: fruit purée (see method)**

Cream the butter and sugar until soft. Beat in the eggs. Fold in the sifted flour and salt, add the milk. Grease 8 shallow oven-proof dishes or pans well and heat; then spoon in the batter. Bake for 10–15 minutes towards the top of a hot oven, 425°F. Serve with hot fruit purée; apple, cherry, raspberry, apricot and blueberry are ideal.

Cheese Pudding with Mixed Vegetables, Treacle Tart

SAUTÉ POTATOES

¾–1 lb. cooked potatoes · little fat · chopped parsley

Slice the potatoes neatly. Fry in the hot fat until golden on both sides. Drain on absorbent paper, top with parsley.

APPLE LEMON MOLD

2 lemons · 2½ cups hot *thick* apple purée ·
2 envelopes unflavored gelatin ·
2½ tablespoons corn syrup · lemon slices

Apple Lemon Mold

Stir the grated rind of the lemons into the hot apple purée. Soften the powdered gelatin in the juice from the lemons. Stir into the hot apple purée with the corn syrup. Spoon into a rinsed mold and allow to set. Turn out, decorate with lemon slices and serve with ice cream or cream.

This menu is designed to turn a very simple one-course family meal into a special one for an increased number of people, i.e. 6–8. The Salad Niçoise makes the meat 'go further'.

SALAD NIÇOISE

1 can (8 oz.) tuna fish · 1 can (2 oz.) anchovy fillets ·
lettuce · 3 tomatoes · 2 hard-cooked eggs ·
½ lb. cooked new potatoes (optional) ·
½ lb. cooked beans (optional) ·
mayonnaise or oil and vinegar · seasoning ·
few black and green olives (optional)

Dice the tuna fish and separate the anchovy fillets. Make a
salad of lettuce, tomatoes and hard-cooked eggs. Add sliced
cooked new potatoes and cooked beans when available.
Add the tuna fish and the anchovy fillets. Toss in either
mayonnaise or well-seasoned oil and vinegar. The salad
may be garnished with black or green olives.
To vary: Add capers or chopped gherkins.

LIVER AND STEAK CASSEROLE

*This is an excellent way of adding liver to a menu. Many people
dislike liver, which is a pity, as it is such a nutritious meat,
but in this casserole the flavor is not too strong. If you add a little
brown sugar and orange juice to the brown stock this takes
away any bitter taste.*

½ lb. calf's liver · 1 lb. boneless chuck steak ·
seasoning · ¼ cup flour · ¼ cup margarine ·
2½ cups brown stock ·
1½ tablespoons tomato paste ·
2 teaspoons Worcestershire sauce · 8 small onions ·
¼ lb. button mushrooms · chopped parsley

Cut the liver and steak into small pieces. Coat in seasoned
flour and fry in the margarine. Gradually add the stock plus
the tomato paste and Worcestershire sauce. Cover the pan
and simmer for about 1½ hours. Add the peeled onions and
the mushrooms, then continue cooking for a further ¾–1 hour
until the steak is tender. Top with chopped parsley. *The
casserole serves 4–6 normally, but with the salad could serve
8 people.*

Planning wisely: Warm the oranges before you halve and
squeeze out the juice – you will have a bigger yield of juice.
If you have no small onions for the Liver and Steak Casserole
use pickled onions instead; they give a very good flavor to the
dish. When you have time, it is a good idea to chop several
tablespoons of parsley and store it in a covered container in the
refrigerator.

Salad Niçoise

A simple mixed hors d'oeuvre turns an ordinary family meal into a special one. It need not be too expensive, and can often incorporate left-over ingredients, such as cooked rice and potatoes, small quantities of salad ingredients and left-over fish and meat. A roast is a good choice for a family meal as it is always popular and requires little preparation. If you buy a fairly large roast, as suggested in the recipe below, it will give you plenty to have cold.

MIXED HORS D'OEUVRE

Rice and pepper salad: Mix $\frac{1}{2}$ cup cooked rice with 1 chopped green pepper and a little onion. Toss in oil and vinegar dressing and top with chopped parsley.

Shrimp eggs: Hard-cook 3 eggs, halve, remove the yolks and mash with mayonnaise. Add a few chopped shrimp, pile into the white cases and top with whole shrimp.

Tomato slices: Toss 3–4 sliced tomatoes in a little oil, vinegar, seasoning and finely chopped onion. Top with chopped parsley.

Sardines: Lightly season canned sardines and sprinkle with lemon juice and chopped parsley.

Onions and cream: Slice 2 onions into rings. Toss in a little light cream, sour cream or yogurt and season. Top with paprika or chopped parsley.

Diced cucumber: Toss peeled and diced cucumber in a little oil, vinegar, seasoning and chopped chives.

APRICOT STUFFED PORK

about $4\frac{1}{2}$ lb. loin of pork ·
1 cup fresh breadcrumbs, preferably wholewheat ·
$\frac{1}{4}$ cup melted margarine ·
$\frac{3}{4}$ cup chopped canned or cooked apricots ·
$\frac{1}{2}$ cup raisins ·
1–$2\frac{1}{2}$ tablespoons slivered almonds (optional) ·
seasoning · 1 tablespoon chopped parsley ·
little apricot syrup · little oil

Have the pork boned so it can be rolled round the stuffing. Blend the crumbs with the melted margarine, apricots, raisins, almonds, seasoning, chopped parsley and apricot syrup. Cooking time includes the weight of the stuffing so allow about 2 hours. Brush the fat with a little oil. Start in a hot oven, 425–450°F, and reduce the heat to moderately hot, 400°F, after about 45 minutes. Roast potatoes in hot fat in a separate pan.

APPLE SAUCE

1 lb. apples · little water · sugar

Simmer peeled sliced apples in a little water with sugar to taste. Blend until a smooth purée.

FRUIT PIE

$1\frac{1}{2}$–2 lb. fruit* · water · sugar to taste · short crust or flaky pastry made with $1\frac{1}{2}$–2 cups flour, etc. (see pages 71 and 116) · granulated or confectioners' sugar
Choose fairly tart fruit to follow the rather rich flavored pork, e.g. plums, rhubarb, currants or gooseberries.

Prepare and put the fruit in the pie dish. Add the minimum of water and a little sugar. Top with short crust or flaky pastry. Bake for about 40–45 minutes until the pastry is crisp and brown and the fruit soft. Reduce the heat or lay a piece of foil over the pastry if it is becoming too brown. Sprinkle with sugar before serving.

Planning wisely: Make the hors d'oeuvre earlier and put this, on its platter, in the refrigerator or a cool place. Cover very lightly with damped kitchen paper and it will stay fresh-looking for 2–3 hours. If you make a quantity of fresh crumbs, when you have a little time, store them in jars or polythene boxes in a cool place or in the refrigerator or freezer, then you can remove the quantity required for the apricot stuffing or any other stuffings.

PINEAPPLE MEAT CAKES

1 large onion · 1 clove garlic (optional) ·
$\frac{1}{4}$ cup margarine or fat · 1 lb. sausagemeat · 1 egg ·
seasoning · 4 pineapple rings · 1–2 tomatoes

Peel and chop the onion and garlic finely. Heat the margarine or fat in a pan. Gently sauté the onion and garlic until soft. Blend with the sausagemeat, egg and a little extra seasoning if desired. Form into 8 flat cakes. Fry or broil until the sausagemeat is cooked (about 10–12 minutes). Sandwich 2 cakes together with a ring of pineapple. Top with rings of uncooked tomato. Serve with grilled tomatoes.

Planning wisely: Keep a container of dehydrated (dried) onion in the house and use this as the instructions on the package when you are short of time – it saves chopping a fresh onion. Use garlic salt instead of crushed garlic.

To vary: Use 1 lb. ground meat instead of sausagemeat; this can be ground beef, lamb or lean pork. If the meat is raw prepare and cook as the recipe above, but if the meat is already cooked you will need to add a little thick sauce and crumbs to make it bind together. Sauté the onion and garlic in the margarine or fat (as above), blend in 2 tablespoons flour and cook for 2–3 minutes. Stir in 6 tablespoons stock or milk, bring to the boil slowly, stirring all the time. Add 1 lb. ground cooked meat, $\frac{1}{3}$ cup breadcrumbs, 1 egg and seasoning. Form into 8 cakes and cook for about 6 minutes only, do not over-cook.

Mixed Hors d'Oeuvre, Apricot Stuffed Pork with Apple Sauce, Roast Potatoes and Brussels Sprouts, Fruit Pie

Casserole Menus

The menus that follow are for dishes to be cooked in covered containers in the oven. If you have insufficient casseroles use cake pans with fixed, not loose, bases or oven-proof dishes. Cover the pans or dishes with foil. If the recipe contains an appreciable amount of liquid it can spoil the cake tin slightly, causing the cake mixture to stick. To avoid this, grease tins very well after use as a casserole. All menus in this chapter serve 4 unless stated otherwise.

MENU

**CHICKEN AND AVOCADO CASSEROLE
WITH BAKED POTATOES,
PEAS AND CARROTS
HAWAIIAN NUT PUDDING
BAKED CHEESE FINGERS**

Set the oven at moderate to moderately hot, 375–400°F. Allow about 1 hour for the chicken dish with vegetables, 45 minutes for the pudding, and about 15 minutes for the cheese fingers. This menu serves 6.

CHICKEN AND AVOCADO CASSEROLE

**6 legs and thighs of young chicken · seasoning ·
¼ cup flour ·
¼ teaspoon dried, or 1 teaspoon fresh chopped, thyme ·**
**1 lemon · 6 tablespoons butter · 2 onions ·
1¼ cups dry white wine ·
½ cup chicken stock or water and ½ chicken bouillon cube · 1 tablespoon flour · ½ cup heavy cream ·
2 ripe avocados · little oil**

Coat the chicken in the seasoned flour, mixed with the dried or fresh thyme and the very finely grated lemon rind. Brown in 4 tablespoons of the butter then put into a casserole. Add the remaining butter to the pan. Toss the sliced onions in this for a few minutes, add the white wine and chicken stock or water and bouillon cube, blended with the flour. Bring to the boil and cook until thickened. Pour over the chicken. Cover and cook for nearly 1 hour in a fairly hot part of the oven. Remove from the oven, cool slightly so the liquid is no longer boiling, stir in the cream. Slice the peeled pears and sprinkle with the lemon juice. Put on top of the chicken and brush with a little oil. Return to the coolest part of oven for 10 minutes.

Dice 1 lb. carrots and mix with ½ lb. fresh or frozen peas in a casserole. Cover with cold water, add salt. Cover and cook in a fairly hot part of the oven.

HAWAIIAN NUT PUDDING

**6 oranges · 1 medium-sized can pineapple rings ·
¼ cup butter · ¼ cup sugar ·
juice 1 fresh orange or 2 tablespoons Curaçao ·
½ cup chopped nuts**

Cut away the peel from the oranges. Strain the syrup from
the pineapple and measure out 10 tablespoons. Stand each
orange on a ring of canned pineapple and put into a casserole.
Heat the butter in a pan, add the sugar, and stir until the
sugar has dissolved. Add the pineapple syrup and orange
juice or Curaçao. Pour into the casserole and cover. Bake
in the coolest part of the oven. Lift out and cover the oranges
with chopped nuts.

BAKED CHEESE FINGERS

**12 fingers bread and butter ·
sliced Cheddar or Gruyère cheese · 1 egg ·
seasoning · 5 tablespoons milk ·
Garnish: watercress**

Make sandwiches with the fingers of bread and butter and
the sliced cheese. Beat the egg with seasoning and milk.
Dip the sandwiches in this and arrange in a shallow buttered
casserole. Bake in the coolest part of the oven. Garnish with
watercress.

*Chicken and Avocado Casserole with Baked Potatoes, Peas
and Carrots*

Set the oven at moderate, 350–375°F, for 1 hour for the risotto and eggplant dishes and about 1¼ hours for the pudding. This menu serves 4–6.

OVEN-BAKED RISOTTO

2½ tablespoons oil · 1 clove garlic · 2 onions ·
1 green pepper · ¼ lb. mushrooms ·
1½ cups long grain rice ·
3 cups chicken stock or water and 3 chicken bouillon cubes · seasoning · 2–3 oz. white raisins ·
¼ lb. chicken livers or calf's liver ·
Topping: chopped parsley, grated cheese

Heat the oil in a pan, toss in the crushed garlic, peeled sliced onions, diced green pepper and sliced mushrooms. Add the rice, chicken stock or water and bouillon cubes, seasoning, white raisins and diced chicken livers or calf's liver. Bring the stock to the boil then spoon the mixture into a deep casserole. Wrap foil around the outside of the casserole to be certain the rice does not dry. Cover tightly. Put into the coolest part of the oven. Spoon out of the casserole on to a hot serving dish. Top with chopped parsley and lots of grated cheese.
To vary: Add diced cooked ham or bacon in place of the chicken or calf's liver. Use different vegetables.

EGGPLANT AND TOMATOES AU GRATIN

2 large eggplants · 1 lb. tomatoes · seasoning ·
2½ tablespoons melted butter ·
Topping: breadcrumbs, preferably brown ·
little butter

Slice very thinly, but do not skin, the eggplants and tomatoes. Put one third of the tomatoes in the casserole, season well. Add half the eggplants, seasoning, 1 tablespoon melted butter, half the remaining tomatoes, the rest of the eggplants, seasoning, butter and the last of the tomatoes. Top with a thick layer of crumbs and a little butter. Put on a lid that does not press down over the crumbs or leave the dish uncovered for a very crisp topping. Bake in the coolest part of the oven.

RHUBARB AND DATE PUDDING

6 tablespoons margarine · 1½ cups self-rising or all-purpose flour, sifted with 1½ teaspoons baking powder · ½ cup sugar · 1 egg · milk ·
½ lb. chopped uncooked rhubarb ·
¼ lb. pitted chopped dates

Rub the margarine into the flour. Add the sugar, egg and enough milk to make a sticky consistency. Add the rhubarb and dates. Put into a greased 8-inch cake pan or a 5 cup pie dish. Stand in a container of water; the water should be as high as possible in the container, but not so high that it boils over. Put a sheet of foil over both the pudding the container. Cook in the hottest part of the oven. Serve with heavy cream or custard sauce.

Set the oven at moderate to moderately hot, 375–400°F. Allow about 45 minutes for all the menu, except the potatoes which need 25 minutes.

STUFFED ONION CASSEROLE

4 large onions · seasoning ·
1 cup fresh breadcrumbs ·
½ lb. chopped cooked meat* or raw lambs' kidneys ·
2 tablespoons margarine ·
¼ teaspoon dried, or 1 teaspoon chopped fresh, sage ·
1¼ cups brown sauce (see below) ·
small package frozen green beans
*pork and ham are particularly good in this dish

Peel the onions and boil in salted water until nearly soft. Remove from the water, leave till cool enough to handle. Remove the center of each onion, chop finely and mix with the breadcrumbs, chopped meat, margarine, sage and seasoning. Press firmly into the middle of each onion, put into a casserole. Make a little thick brown sauce (see below) from some of the onion liquid in the pan. Pour around the onions, add the green beans (broken up so they can be spread around the onions) and a little extra seasoning. Cover the casserole and cook in the fairly hot part of the oven.

BROWN SAUCE

2 tablespoons fat · ¼ cup flour ·
1¼ cups brown stock or onion stock plus 1 teaspoon beef or yeast extract · seasoning

Heat the fat, stir in the flour and cook for several minutes. Gradually add the stock and beef or yeast extract. Bring to the boil, cook until thickened and season to taste.

DUCHESSE POTATOES

¼ cup margarine · 1–2 egg yolks ·
1 lb. mashed potatoes

Beat the margarine and egg yolks into the mashed potato. Pile in shapes on a greased oven-proof dish, heat and brown in the hottest part of the oven.

COMPÔTE OF FRUIT

1–1½ lb. prepared firm fruit, i.e. apples, plums, pears, gooseberries or use a mixture of fruit · ½ cup sugar ·
½–1¼ cups water

Put the fruit into a casserole. Make a syrup of the sugar and water and pour over the fruit. Put a lid on the casserole and cook in the coolest part of the oven. Turn or switch off the heat when removing the onions and potatoes from the oven. Serve the compôte with heavy cream or custard sauce. If the fruit is fairly tart, i.e. gooseberries, it can be sprinkled with a little brown or demerara sugar just before serving.
To vary: Dried fruit, e.g. apricots and apples, make excellent compôtes. Soak overnight, then cook as above.

casserole. Heat the fat in a pan. Coat the meat whirls in seasoned flour, toss in the hot fat until golden. Lift on top of the vegetables. Blend the brown stock, or water and bouillon cube, with the fat in a pan. Pour around the beef whirls. Cover the casserole and cook in the fairly cool part of the oven. Sprinkle with chopped parsley just before serving.

Set the oven at slow to very moderate, 300–325°F. Allow about 2 hours for the whole menu.

BRAISED BEEF WHIRLS

4 slices round or rump steak · 3 onions ·
⅓ lb. ox kidney · 1 tablespoon chopped parsley ·
2 tablespoons margarine or shredded suet ·
seasoning · 6 large carrots · ¼ cup fat · ¼ cup flour ·
1¼ cups brown stock or water and 1 beef bouillon cube ·
Garnish: chopped parsley

Halve the slices of beef, chop 1 onion and the kidney finely. Mix the onion, kidney, chopped parsley, margarine or suet and seasoning. Divide between the pieces of meat and roll up firmly. Secure with wooden cocktail sticks or string. Peel and slice the remaining onions and the carrots. Put into a

MACEDOINE OF VEGETABLES

4 potatoes · 1 rutabaga · 2 turnips · water · salt ·
little margarine · chopped parsley ·

Peel and dice the vegetables. Put into a casserole. Cover with water, add salt and cover the casserole *tightly*. Cook in the coolest part of the oven. Strain, top with margarine and parsley.

RICE PUDDING DE LUXE

⅓ cup rice · 2 tablespoons sugar · 2½ cups milk ·
½ cup light cream · 3 tablespoons white raisins ·
2 tablespoons halved glacé cherries

Put all the ingredients into a casserole. Cook in the coolest part of the oven until the pudding is creamy and golden brown on top.

Braised Beef Whirls

Set the oven at very moderate to moderate, 325–350°F. The soup takes about a hour, the Lamb Lyonnaise 1¼ hours, the pudding about 1½ hours, but if this is over-cooking reduce the heat when removing the lamb from the oven.

VEGETABLE RICE SOUP

¾–1 lb. mixed vegetables – onions, carrots, tomatoes, turnips ·
3¾ cups hot chicken stock or water and 4 chicken bouillon cubes · *bouquet garni* · seasoning ·
1 tablespoon rice · chopped parsley and/or chives

Choose a really deep casserole so the soup does not boil over. Peel and chop the vegetables fairly finely. Put into the casserole with the hot stock or water and bouillon cubes, the *bouquet garni*, seasoning and rice. Cover and place in a fairly cool part of the oven. Sprinkle the chopped parsley and/or chives over the soup before serving.

LAMB LYONNAISE

1 lb. potatoes · 1 lb. onions · seasoning ·
very little chopped sage or rosemary ·
4 large or 8 smaller thick, *lean* lamb chops ·
½ cup stock or water and ½ bouillon cube (optional) ·
Garnish: sliced raw tomato and/or watercress

Peel and slice the potatoes and onions very thinly. Put half the potatoes and onions into a shallow, preferably long, oven-proof dish. Season very well and top with the sage or rosemary. Put the chops over the potato mixture. Add the rest of the onions then the potatoes and season well. If you like a moist mixture add the stock or water and bouillon cube. Cover the dish tightly and put in the hottest part of the oven. Before serving, garnish with slices of raw tomato and/or watercress. Serve with green salad.
To vary: Put a little fat over the sliced potatoes and lift the lid 40 minutes before serving to allow the potatoes to brown. Add thickly sliced tomatoes to the potatoes and onions. Add sliced, fried eggplant to the potatoes and onions.

APPLE CRUMB PUDDING

¼ cup butter or margarine · ¼ cup brown sugar ·
1 tablespoon corn syrup · 1 teaspoon mixed spice ·
3 cups fresh breadcrumbs ·
grated rind and juice 1 lemon ·
2–3 good-sized cooking apples · ¼ cup sugar ·
½ cup seedless raisins

Cream the butter or margarine, brown sugar and syrup. Add the mixed spice, breadcrumbs and lemon rind. Put half this mixture into a greased casserole. Peel and slice the apples, mix with the sugar, lemon juice and raisins. Put over the crumb mixture, then top with the rest of the crumbs and a foil covering or a lid. Bake in a cool part of the oven. Lift the lid when 'dishing-up' the meat course so the crumbs can crisp. Serve with a syrup sauce (see below).

SYRUP SAUCE

3 tablespoons corn syrup ·
grated rind and juice 1 lemon · ½ cup water

Mix all the ingredients together. Heat in the oven in a small covered casserole.

Set the oven to moderate, 350–375°F. Allow 1¼ hours for the scalloped potatoes, 40 minutes for the fish and 25–30 minutes for the dessert.

PIQUANT FISH CASSEROLE

⅓ lb. mushrooms ·
2 tablespoons margarine or butter ·
1 tablespoon chopped scallion or chives and/or
1 tablespoon chopped parsley ·
½ cup light cream · 2 teaspoons Angostura bitters ·
4 portions or 8 small fillets white fish ·
1 tablespoon butter · seasoning

Slice the mushrooms, toss in the hot margarine or butter. Add the scallion or chives and/or parsley, the cream and Angostura bitters. Put the fish into a buttered casserole, season and spoon the mushroom mixture over the fish. Cover the dish and bake in the coolest part of the oven.

PAPRIKA SCALLOPED POTATOES

1 lb. potatoes · 2 cups milk ·
¼ cup margarine or butter · good pinch salt ·
shake pepper · 1–2 teaspoons paprika

Put the peeled and very thinly sliced potatoes into a 1½–2 quart casserole. Heat the milk with the rest of the ingredients. Pour over the potatoes and cook, uncovered, in a fairly hot part of the oven.
To vary: Omit the paprika and sprinkle the potato layers with chopped herbs: parsley, thyme, rosemary, sage or a mixture.
Layer the potatoes with sliced onions and season lightly between each layer. Reduce the quantity of milk to 1¼ cups.

BANANA AND COCONUT BAKE

2 tablespoons butter · ¼ cup brown sugar ·
juice 2 oranges or ½ cup frozen orange juice ·
4 large or 8 small bananas ·
¼ cup flaked coconut

Heat the butter, sugar and orange juice until the sugar melts. Put the peeled bananas into a casserole. Add the orange liquid and press the coconut over the bananas. Bake in a fairly hot part of the oven.

Above: Vegetable Rice Soup, Lamb Lyonnaise, Apple Crumb Pudding
Below: Piquant Fish Casserole

Meals for Children

These menus are planned for families with small children. No busy mother wants to cook two separate meals, one for the adults and another for young children, but the needs and tastes of grown-ups and children are not necessarily exactly the same. It is, however, often possible to adapt the dishes so they are ideal for all the family; these 'extra' ingredients are given in detail at the end of each dish. Children vary of course; some young children will enjoy adult flavorings so some adaptations may not be necessary.
Quantities given are for 2 adults and 2 young children (who would have smaller portions).

MENU

GRAPE AND MELON COUPE
FRIED LIVER, BACON
AND BROWN GRAVY
CARROTS AND CREAMED POTATOES
CHEESE AND CRACKERS

MENU

SAUSAGE BOATS
WITH BAKED POTATOES
AND CAULIFLOWER
CRISP TOPPED BANANA RICE

GRAPE AND MELON COUPE

¼ lb. grapes · 1 small, or part of a larger, melon ·
½ cup water · 2 tablespoons sugar or honey ·
½ teaspoon ground ginger

Halve the grapes and melon. Remove the seeds from both fruits. Dice the melon and arrange the fruit in 4 glasses. Make a syrup by boiling the water and sugar or honey.
For children. Cool the syrup slightly and spoon a little over the children's portions (unless they like ginger).
For adults. Add the ginger to the remaining syrup and spoon over the adult portions.

FRIED LIVER AND BACON

4 bacon slices · ¾ lb. sliced calf's liver · seasoning ·
flour · little fat if needed · sugar (see method) ·
mustard (see method)

Fry slices of bacon for *all* the family *lightly* so they do not over-cook while being kept waiting. Coat the liver with a *very little* seasoned flour and fry in the pan until tender. If the bacon fat is inadequate, add a little extra fat before putting the liver into the pan so it does not dry out. Remove from the pan when cooked and make a brown gravy.
For children. Liver is such an important food that it is worth taking a little trouble to ensure children enjoy it. Liver has a slightly bitter taste, which children may not like, so add a little sugar to the flour coating. When the gravy is made, you can also add a pinch of sugar to part of this. Presentation is important to children, so form part of the creamed potatoes into 2 'nests'. Chop the bacon and liver, pile into the 'nests' and top with gravy.
For adults The gravy can be made more piquant for adults by adding a little prepared mustard or Worcestershire sauce.

SAUSAGE BOATS

6–8 large sausages ·
6–8 very thin slices fresh bread ·
¼ cup margarine ·
mustard and/or cottage or cream cheese
(see method) ·
Garnish: watercress and tomatoes

Cook the sausages. Spread one side of the bread with margarine. Put a sausage in the center, gather up the sides to form a 'boat' shape and secure with a wooden cocktail stick. Brush the outside of the bread with melted margarine and crisp in a hot oven, 425–450°F. Garnish with watercress and tomatoes.
For children. Bake really small potatoes, otherwise the meal is too 'solid'. Make the cauliflower look attractive by topping with a little paprika and a chopped hard-cooked egg.
For adults. Spread bread with mustard and/or cottage cheese.

CRISP TOPPED BANANA RICE

rice pudding (see below) · bananas · brown sugar

Make a creamy rice pudding, or use a canned rice pudding. Put into an oven-proof dish and heat gently. Top with sliced bananas and brown sugar and broil slowly until the sugar bubbles.

RICE PUDDING

Put approximately ⅓ cup rice, ⅓ cup sugar and 2½ cups milk into an oven-proof dish. Cook very slowly for several hours.

Sausage Boats with Baked Potatoes and Cauliflower, Crisp Topped Banana Rice

Cheese and Bacon Kebabs, Blackcurrant Flummery

CHEESE AND BACON KEBABS

4–5 bacon slices · ½ lb. firm Cheddar cheese ·
1–2 ripe eating apples and/or ½ green pepper, ·
few mushrooms · par-boiled onions (see method)

Cut each bacon slice in half. Cut the cheese into cubes, then roll the bacon around the cheese. Put the bacon rolls on to a metal skewer.

For children. Add segments of ripe eating apple.

For adults. Either add apple as above or add rings of green pepper, small mushrooms and tiny onions (brushed with melted fat).

Cook under the broiler, turning round until the bacon is evenly cooked. Do not overcook the cheese as it then becomes less easily digested. Serve on a bed of diced cooked vegetables.

BLACKCURRANT FLUMMERY

1 package (3 oz.) lemon jello · 1¼ cups boiling water ·
2½–4 tablespoons blackcurrant syrup ·
1¼ cups evaporated milk ·
Decoration: 4 slices crystallized lemon

Dissolve the jello in the boiling water. Cool slightly, then add the blackcurrant syrup. Allow to cool and begin to stiffen *very slightly* then spoon into a large bowl. Gradually beat the evaporated milk into the mixture. Pile into 4 glasses and leave to set. Decorate with slices of crystallized lemon.

For adults. If the flavor of this dessert is too bland, put half the blackcurrant mixture into one bowl and the rest into a second bowl. Beat ½ cup evaporated milk into half the jelly and 10 tablespoons yogurt into the remainder.

To vary: Use an orange gelatin and the juice of a fresh orange.

BUTTERSCOTCH RAISIN PUDDING

6 tablespoons brown sugar · 2 tablespoons butter ·
2 cups milk · ½ cup raisins · 1 cup fresh breadcrumbs ·
2 eggs

Put the sugar and butter into a pan, stir over a low heat until the sugar has dissolved. Cool slightly, then add the milk. Heat gently until the milk absorbs the butterscotch. Pour over the raisins and breadcrumbs. Leave for about 20 minutes to soften the crumbs, then add the well-beaten eggs. Pour into

Salmon Fish Cakes

a pie dish, stand in a container of water and bake for about 1 hour in the center of a slow to very moderate oven, 300–325°F.

For children. This dessert should be popular with children as well as being nutritious.

For adults. The dessert may be too insipid, so serve with lemon flavored yogurt, i.e. add grated lemon rind and juice to plain yogurt.

MENU

SALMON FISH CAKES WITH CHEESE SAUCE AND CREAMED SPINACH DATE AND NUT PIE

SALMON FISH CAKES

2 eggs · 1 can (16 oz.) salmon ·
¾ lb. potatoes, mashed · seasoning ·
2 tablespoons flour · ½ cup dry breadcrumbs ·
4–6 tablespoons fat for frying (optional) ·
capers and anchovy essence (see method)

Separate the egg yolks from the whites. Flake the salmon and mix with the potato. Blend with the egg yolks and seasoning. Form into flat cakes, dust with seasoned flour. Brush with the egg whites and coat with the breadcrumbs. Fry in a little hot fat, or bake for about 15 minutes on a well-greased and heated cookie tray in a moderately hot oven, 400°F, or 25 minutes in a moderate oven, 375°F. Serve with a cheese sauce and chopped or sieved cooked spinach, blended with some light cream.

For children or adults. Fried food is less easily digested, so bake.

For adults. Blend 1–2 teaspoons capers and a little anchovy essence with some of the fish and potato mixture.

DATE AND NUT PIE

¾ cup semolina (farina) · ¾ cup all-purpose flour ·
½ cup sugar ·
6 tablespoons melted butter or margarine ·
½ lb. pitted dates · 3¾ tablespoons boiling water ·
2½ tablespoons honey ·
1 tablespoon orange or lemon juice ·
2 medium-sized apples ·
chopped walnuts (see method)

Blend the semolina (farina) and flour. Add the sugar and melted butter or margarine. Chop the dates and put into a bowl. Add the boiling water, honey, orange or lemon juice and the peeled and grated apples. Stir together until smooth. Sprinkle half the semolina mixture in the bottom of a 7-inch shallow oven-proof dish. Add the date mixture.

Top the date or date and nut mixture with the rest of the semolina mixture. Bake in the center of a moderate oven, 375°F, for 35–40 minutes. Reduce the heat after 20 minutes if the topping is becoming too brown.

For adults. Spread a generous quantity of coarsely chopped walnuts over part of the date mixture. These are not very suitable for small children.

BEEF DARIOLES

¼ cup fat · 1–2 onions · ¼ cup flour ·
½ cup canned tomato juice · ¾ lb.–1 lb. ground beef ·
½ cup fresh breadcrumbs · seasoning ·
Tomato Sauce: ¼ cup flour ·
2 cups canned tomato juice ·
2 tablespoons margarine · seasoning ·
1–2 teaspoons capers and few drops Tabasco sauce
(see method)

Heat the fat and fry the finely chopped or grated onions for a few minutes. Stir in the flour and cook for several minutes. Gradually add the tomato juice. Bring the tomato mixture to the boil and cook until thickened. Stir in the ground beef, breadcrumbs and seasoning. Put into 8 greased small molds. Cover with waxed paper or foil and steam for 30 minutes. Meanwhile, make the tomato sauce. Blend the flour with the tomato juice. Put into a pan with the margarine and seasoning. Bring to the boil and cook until thickened.
For adults. Add the capers and Tabasco to the sauce.

HOT COLESLAW

1 small cabbage · salt ·
1 teaspoon caraway seeds and butter (see method)

Cook the finely shredded cabbage in the minimum of salted water for a very short time so it retains its crisp texture. Children often enjoy very crisp cabbage and it retains more mineral salts and vitamins.
For adults. Try the Continental 'trick' of adding caraway seeds and a lump of butter to the hot cabbage.

SAVORY RICE

1 cup long grain rice · 2 cups water ·
½ teaspoon salt ·
cheese and/ or white raisins (see method)

Put the rice, water and salt into the pan. Bring to the boil, stir briskly, cover the pan, lower the heat and simmer for 15 minutes.
For children. A sprinkling of grated cheese and/or a few white raisins will make the rice more interesting.

ORANGE COFFEE CREAM

2 eggs · 2 tablespoons sugar · 1¼ cups warm milk ·
1 can mandarin oranges ·
1 tablespoon very strong coffee ·
1 envelope unflavored gelatin · heavy cream

Beat the eggs with the sugar. Beat in the warm milk. Cook in the top of a double boiler over hot water, stirring occasionally, until the custard thickens enough to coat the back of a wooden spoon. Meanwhile, blend the syrup from the can of oranges with the coffee. Put the well-drained oranges on one side for the topping. Soften the gelatin in 2 tablespoons of the orange mixture. Heat the rest of the liquid, add the gelatin and stir until dissolved. Allow both the gelatin mixture and the custard to cool, then beat together. Put into a mold that has been rinsed in cold water. Chill until set. Turn out and top with mandarin oranges and whipped cream.
For children. The blending of flavors is delicious and should be popular with all the family. Do not give the children any, or too much, whipped cream topping.

CHICKEN CHARLOTTE

5–6 slices bread ·
¼ cup margarine or butter for frying ·
2 tablespoons margarine or butter · ¼ cup flour ·
just over 1¼ cups milk, or milk and chicken stock ·
about ¾ lb. diced cooked chicken and
¼ lb. diced cooked lean ham, or use all chicken ·
chives and/or lemon thyme (see method) ·
Garnish: parsley

Cut the slices of bread into fingers. Do not cut away the crusts. Fry the bread fingers in the hot margarine or butter until crisp and golden. Drain on absorbent paper. Make a white sauce with the margarine or butter, flour and milk, or milk and chicken stock. Add the chicken and ham. Put half the bread fingers into an oven-proof dish, top with the sauce mixture, then the rest of the fried bread fingers. Heat in the oven for a few minutes. Garnish with parsley.
For adults. Put part of the chicken and ham mixture at one end of the dish for the children. Add chopped chives and/or chopped lemon thyme to the remaining sauce to make the mixture more piquant.
To vary: Use 1 lb. white fish in place of the chicken.

STUFFED TOMATOES

4 large or 8 smaller tomatoes · seasoning ·
½ cup cooked peas
and/or ½ cup cooked sweet corn

Halve the tomatoes, scoop out the pulp, season and mix with the peas and/or sweet corn. Pile into the tomato cases. When tomatoes are at their best serve cold, or heat for a short time only.
For children. If the children are very small, purée the tomato pulp to avoid the seeds.

FRESH FRUIT SALAD

Encourage children to enjoy raw fruit. Adapt the fruits in the salad to the children's taste. Do not over-sweeten.
For children. Moisten with a little fresh orange juice.
For adults. Moisten with a little white wine, or kirsch for special occasions.

Chicken Charlotte with Stuffed Tomatoes, Fresh Fruit Salad

Packed Meals and Picnics

There are many occasions when one needs to take a packed meal. Perhaps you are travelling, and do not wish to break your journey; or maybe it is a family picnic for a day on the beach or in the country. I have added suggestions for Barbecue Meals also where applicable.

All menus in this chapter serve 4 unless stated otherwise.

MENU

TOMATO CREAM SOUP
CHICKEN AND NUT GALANTINE
WITH ROLLS AND BUTTER
FRUIT COLESLAW
CHEESE
This menu serves 5–6

TOMATO CREAM SOUP

3 tablespoons butter or margarine ·
small bunch scallions · 1½ lb. ripe tomatoes ·
seasoning · 1–2 teaspoons brown sugar ·
1¼ cups chicken stock (see Chicken and Nut Galantine below) · little chopped parsley · cream

Heat the butter or margarine. Gently sauté the chopped scallions, then add the peeled chopped tomatoes, seasoning, brown sugar, chicken stock and parsley. Simmer for 10 minutes. Purée. Reheat and put into a warmed thermos or chill and put into a cool thermos. Take cream separately and use a spoonful to top each portion.

CHICKEN AND NUT GALANTINE

1 medium-sized roasting chicken ·
the chicken giblets · 2½ cups water · seasoning ·
1 cup chopped nuts ·
1 cup fresh breadcrumbs, preferably brown · 2 eggs

Cut all the meat from the chicken. Put the bones and giblets into a pan with the water and seasoning. Cover the pan and simmer for 1 hour. Grind the chicken with the meat from the cooked giblets, and add the nuts, breadcrumbs, eggs and ½ cup of the chicken stock. Season well. Put into a well-greased 2 lb. loaf pan, cover with waxed foil or paper. Stand in a container with a little cold water. Bake for 1¼–1½ hours in the center of a very moderate to moderate oven, 325–350°F.

FRUIT COLESLAW

1 small cabbage heart · ½ cup raisins ·
2 dessert apples · 1–2 oranges · mayonnaise

Shred the cabbage, put into a bowl and add the raisins, the peeled diced apples, peeled diced oranges and enough mayonnaise to moisten. Put into a polythene box, cover, and keep in a cool place.

MENU

ORANGE AND TOMATO JUICE COCKTAILS
CHEF'S SALAD
OLD FASHIONED GINGERBREAD
WITH CREAM CHEESE
This menu serves 5–6

ORANGE AND TOMATO JUICE COCKTAILS

Mix 1¼ cups orange juice and 2½ cups tomato juice. Put into a thermos with crushed ice.

CHEF'S SALAD

¼ lb. ham · ⅓ lb. tongue · ¾ lb. chicken ·
⅓ lb. Gruyère cheese · lettuce · 4 tomatoes ·
3 hard-cooked eggs · mayonnaise

Cut the cooked meats and cheese into matchstick pieces, mix well, then put on top of shredded lettuce and sliced tomatoes. Top with quartered eggs. Carry the mayonnaise separately.

OLD FASHIONED GINGERBREAD

2 cups all-purpose flour · ¾ teaspoon baking soda ·
½–1 teaspoon ground cinnamon ·
1½–2 teaspoons ground ginger ·
½ cup butter or shortening ·
¾ cup moist brown sugar · ½ cup molasses · 2 eggs ·
5 tablespoons milk

Sift the dry ingredients. Melt the butter or shortening with the sugar and molasses, add to the flour. Beat in the eggs and milk. Put into an 8-inch square pan lined with waxed paper. Bake for 1¼ hours in the center of a slow to very moderate oven, 300–325°F. Cool in the pan.

Tomato Cream Soup, Chicken and Nut Galantine, Fruit Coleslaw

MENU

SAUSAGE ROLLS (see page 116)
TOMATOES, LETTUCE
ROLLS, BUTTER, CHEESE
HOME-MADE LEMONADE

HOME-MADE LEMONADE

6 lemons · 2½ cups water · about ½ cup sugar ·
ice cubes · extra water or soda water ·
Decoration: sliced lemon · mint

Grate the rind from the lemons. Be careful to take just the top 'zest', i.e. the yellow part of the skin; avoid using the white pith. Squeeze out the juice. Put the water and sugar into a pan. Add the lemon rind. Stir over a low heat until the sugar has dissolved, then boil for a few minutes. Cool, add the lemon juice. This is a concentrated lemonade, so it must be diluted.

Crush the ice cubes finely (never put large ice cubes into a thermos, they could crack the lining). Add the strained lemonade. If you wish to dilute this with water, pour the water into the thermos (use about one-quarter concentrated lemonade and three-quarters water). If you wish to dilute with soda water, simply put the concentrated lemonade into

Green Pepper and Shrimp Cocktails

the thermos with crushed ice and take bottles of soda water. Top the glasses or jug with lemon slices or mint or put these into the thermos to give a stronger flavor.

MENU

GREEN PEPPER AND SHRIMP COCKTAILS
BACON AND EGG PIE (see page 73)
MIXED SALAD
ICED COFFEE

GREEN PEPPER AND SHRIMP COCKTAILS

⅓ lb. shelled shrimp · 3¾ tablespoons mayonnaise ·
1 large green pepper · 2–3 sticks celery · lettuce

Mix the shrimp, mayonnaise, diced green pepper (discard core and seeds) and the chopped celery. Put into a wide-necked thermos or covered container. Wash and shred the lettuce, and carry in a separate container. This salad is highly perishable, so chill until ready to serve.

ICED COFFEE

Put crushed ice into a thermos, cover with cold strong coffee and milk. A little cream can be added or can be taken separately to top the coffee.

Farmhouse Pie

MENU

FARMHOUSE PIE
HAM AND POTATO SALAD
MIXED SALAD
FRUIT SALAD WITH CREAM
This menu serves 6

FARMHOUSE PIE

Savory short crust pastry: 3 cups all-purpose flour ·
good pinch each of salt, celery and garlic salts,
mustard and mixed dried herbs · shake pepper ·
¾ cup margarine or shortening · water to bind ·
Filling: 2 onions · 3 large tomatoes ·
¼ cup margarine · 1 lb. cooked or canned tongue* ·
seasoning · 1–2 tablespoons sweet pickle or chutney ·
beaten egg to glaze
*or tongue mixed with diced cooked chicken

Make the pastry: sieve the flour with the seasonings and herbs.
Rub the margarine or shortening into the flour until the
mixture resembles fine breadcrumbs. Bind with water. Roll
out and use about three-quarters to line a 2 lb. loaf pan. Fry
the peeled and chopped onions and tomatoes in the margarine.
Blend with the diced tongue or tongue and chicken. Season
and add the sweet pickle or chutney. Put into the pastry-lined
pan. Damp the pastry edges with a little water. Roll out the
remainder of the pastry, make a 'lid' to fit on the pie and a few
pastry 'leaves'. Place the lid in position, flute the edges
together. Brush the top of the pie with beaten egg, put the
'leaves' in position and brush these with egg. Make 1 or 2

slits on top for the steam to escape. Bake the pie in the center
of a hot oven, 425–450°F, for about 20 minutes, then lower
the heat to very moderate, 325°F, for a further 20 minutes.
This is good hot or cold.

To make short crust pastry
Use half fat to flour, i.e. 2 cups all-purpose flour and ½ cup
margarine or other fat.
Sieve the flour with a pinch of salt. Rub in the fat until the
mixture looks like fine breadcrumbs. Bind with cold water to
a rolling consistency. 8 oz. pastry means pastry made with
2 cups flour, etc. – *not* 8 oz. completed pastry.

HAM AND POTATO SALAD

1 or 2 thick slices cooked or boiled ham ·
¾–1 lb. cooked potatoes · chopped parsley ·
little grated onion · up to ½ cup mayonnaise ·
chopped chives

Dice the ham, mix with the diced potatoes, chopped parsley,
grated onion and mayonnaise. Put into a polythene box and
top with chopped chives.

To carry salads
Use polythene boxes or bags, foil or a wide-necked thermos.
Wash green salad vegetables, shake dry. Pack at once and
keep cool for as long as possible.

How to make and carry fruit salads
Blend fresh fruits with canned fruit and the syrup from the
can. If using all fresh fruit make a syrup by boiling a little
sugar and water, flavor with orange or lemon juice. Put the
fruit and syrup into polythene containers, with a well-fitting
seal, or into screw-topped jars or wide-necked thermos.

SEAFOOD SALAD

½ cup long grain rice · ½ teaspoon salt ·
7½ tablespoons mayonnaise · ¼ cup cooked peas ·
¼ cup cooked sweet corn · 1 small can tuna or salmon ·
½ cup shrimp or cooked or canned crabmeat ·
piece cucumber · lettuce

Boil the rice in salted water until just tender. Drain, toss in the mayonnaise while the rice is still hot. Cool. Blend with the cooked peas and sweet corn, flaked tuna or salmon, chopped shrimp or flaked crabmeat and diced cucumber. Carry the lettuce separately. As the fish is highly perishable, this salad should be carried in a container in an insulated bag or in a wide-necked thermos.

FRIED CHICKEN DRUMSTICKS

4 chicken drumsticks · seasoning · ¼ cup flour ·
1 egg · ½ cup dry breadcrumbs · fat for frying

Skin and coat the chicken drumsticks with seasoned flour then beaten egg and breadcrumbs. Fry until the chicken is cooked, crisp and golden brown. Drain on absorbent paper.
Barbecue tip: Do not cook the chicken at home, but over the barbecue fire. It is not necessary to coat the joints. Simply brush with oil or melted butter, flavored with a little prepared mustard and a few drops Worcestershire or chili sauce. Cook sausages, tomatoes and baked potatoes, wrap the French bread in foil and heat over the barbecue fire.

CHEDDAR SCOTCH EGGS

4 eggs · ¾ cup grated Cheddar cheese ·
2 tablespoons butter · seasoning · ¾ lb. sausagemeat ·
¼ cup flour · 1 egg · ½ cup dry breadcrumbs ·
deep fat for frying

Hard-cook the eggs, shell and halve. Remove the yolks very carefully, mash, then add the grated cheese, butter and seasoning. Mix well and press back again into the white cases. Put the halves together, then coat each egg in about ¼ of the sausagemeat. Make sure the sausagemeat covers the eggs completely. Roll in seasoned flour, then beaten egg and breadcrumbs. Fry in hot fat until crisp and brown, and the sausagemeat is cooked. Drain on absorbent paper then wrap.

SHORTBREAD FLAPJACKS

¼ cup butter · 2 tablespoons sugar ·
1 cup all-purpose flour · milk to bind ·
Topping: 3 tablespoons butter or margarine ·
¼ cup brown sugar · 1 tablespoon corn syrup ·
2 cups rolled oats

Cream the butter and sugar, add the flour and enough milk to bind; add as little milk as possible. Press out to an 8-inch round. Put into a greased cake pan with a loose base or on a flat cookie tray. To make the flapjack topping, melt the butter or margarine with the brown sugar and syrup in a fairly large pan. Add the rolled oats and blend well. Spoon the flapjack mixture on top of the shortbread. Spread flat with the back of a damp metal spoon or palette knife. Bake in the center of a very moderate to moderate oven, 325–350°F, for about 30 minutes. Mark into sections while warm. Cool in or on the tin. Carry in a polythene box or tin.
Barbecue tip: Warm the Cheddar Scotch Eggs over the barbecue fire and serve with a spicy sauce. To make this, blend 3¾ tablespoons kechup, 1¼ tablespoons Worcestershire sauce, 1¼ tablespoons vinegar, 2 teaspoons brown sugar and 1 teaspoon prepared mustard. Spoon over each egg just before serving.
Bake apples over the barbecue fire and serve with hot syrup flavored with ginger or lemon juice.

COUNTRY BURGERS

2–3 slices bacon · 2 tablespoons fat · 1 onion ·
¼ lb. mushrooms · ¾ lb. corned beef ·
1 cup fresh breadcrumbs · seasoning ·
pinch dried mixed herbs or teaspoon chopped fresh herbs · 2 oz. potato chips · buttered rolls or lettuce

Chop the bacon very finely, fry in a pan with the fat until nearly crisp. Add the grated onion and chopped mushrooms. Mix with the flaked corned beef, breadcrumbs, seasoning and herbs. Form the mixture into 8 flat cakes. Roll in the crushed potato chips, then allow to cool. Put in halved soft buttered rolls or between lettuce leaves.

DATE AND NUT FINGERS

½ lb. sugar cookies · finely grated rind 1 lemon ·
1¼ tablespoons lemon juice · 1 cup chopped nuts ·
¼ lb. pitted chopped dates ·
up to ½ cup sweetened condensed milk ·
confectioners' sugar for topping·

Crush the cookies and put into a mixing bowl. Add the lemon rind, lemon juice, chopped nuts and dates. Mix well, then add up to ½ cup condensed milk to bind. Coat an 8-inch cake pan with sugar. Put in the mixture, smooth and top with sugar. Leave for several hours in the refrigerator to set. Carry in the tin, cut into fingers.

Seafood Salad, Barbecued Chicken Drumsticks and Sausages

Hot Weather Menus

Most of us enjoy hot weather but it can have a disastrous effect upon one's appetite. If people are very hot and/or very tired, they often lose their taste for food. It is a sensible idea to have a cool, refreshing drink and relax for a while before eating. Do not make the mistake of having all cold dishes in hot weather, this is boring and monotonous; many hot dishes are light and 'easy to eat'. Avoid food that is very solid and take special care that food looks interesting and inviting. Try to cook meals in the oven, rather than on top of the range; this keeps the kitchen and the cook cool.

All menus in this chapter serve 4 unless stated otherwise.

MENU

**TOMATO JUICE COCKTAIL
SAVORY CHEESE LOG
WITH GARLIC BREAD AND SALAD
PINEAPPLE SOUFFLÉ PUDDING**
This menu serves 4–6

TOMATO JUICE COCKTAIL

2½ cups tomato juice · shake celery salt ·
pinch cayenne pepper · little Worcestershire sauce ·
few bruised mint leaves · 1 egg white ·
very finely chopped mint or parsley

Blend the tomato juice with the celery salt, cayenne pepper, Worcestershire sauce and mint leaves. Chill. Frost 4–6 glasses by brushing the rims with egg white, turning upside down and dipping in very finely chopped mint or parsley. Serve the cocktail in the frosted glasses.

To vary: Add 1 tablespoon chopped chives or parsley to the cocktail. Add about 4 tablespoons very finely chopped celery in place of the celery salt. Garnish with small celery leaves.

SAVORY CHEESE LOG

1–1¼ lb. Cheddar cheese ·
2½–4 tablespoons each of diced cucumber,
sliced stuffed olives, sliced radishes and
chopped walnuts · mayonnaise ·
Garnish: olives, halved walnuts, radishes

Grate the cheese finely. Mix with the cucumber, olives, radishes and walnuts. Moisten with enough mayonnaise to make the consistency of very thick whipped cream. Form into a long roll. Garnish with olives, halved walnuts and radishes, chill well. Serve on a bed of green salad with halved tomatoes, cooked peas (topped with chopped scallions) and sliced cucumber. Serve extra mayonnaise or oil and vinegar dressing separately.

To vary: Other hard cheeses, such as Gruyère, Edam and Jarlsberg, could be used in place of Cheddar.

GARLIC BREAD

1 French loaf · ¼ cup butter ·
garlic salt or crushed garlic

Make ½–¾-inch cuts in the French loaf, almost to the base, then pull gently apart with your hands. Blend the butter with the garlic salt or crushed garlic. Spread a little of the garlic butter in each cut. Wrap in foil and leave for about 10–15 minutes in a moderately hot oven, 400°F, or about 25–30 minutes in a very moderate to moderate oven, 325–350°F.

To vary: Use 1 tablespoon chopped herbs in place of the garlic, i.e. parsley, chives, chervil, rosemary.
Add 1 teaspoon curry powder and 1 tablespoon finely chopped chutney in place of the garlic.
Cream the butter with a few drops of anchovy extract or a few finely chopped anchovies in place of the garlic.
Use 2½ tablespoons very finely chopped onion or scallion in place of the garlic.

PINEAPPLE SOUFFLÉ PUDDING

¼ cup margarine or butter · ¼ cup sugar ·
grated rind and juice 1 lemon · 2 eggs ·
½ cup self-rising flour or all-purpose flour sifted with
½ teaspoon baking powder ·
15 tablespoons canned pineapple juice

Cream the margarine or butter with the sugar and grated lemon rind. Separate the egg yolks from the whites. Gradually beat in the yolks and flour. Add the pineapple and lemon juice. Fold in the stiffly beaten egg whites. The mixture may look curdled at this stage, but it does not matter. Pour into a pie dish, stand this in a container with a little cold water. Bake in the center of a very moderate to moderate oven, 325–350°F, for about 40 minutes. Serve hot. The pudding separates during cooking; you have a sauce layer at the bottom of the dish with a light soufflé mixture on top.

To vary: Serve with rings of hot pineapple or with vanilla ice cream. Use orange juice in place of pineapple juice.

Tomato Juice Cocktail, Savory Cheese Log with Garlic Bread, Pineapple Soufflé Pudding

MUSHROOM VICHYSOISSE

2 large old potatoes · 3 large leeks ·
2½ cups chicken stock or water and 2 chicken bouillon
cubes · 10 button mushrooms · ½ cup light cream ·
seasoning ·
Topping: cream, chopped chives

Peel the potatoes and clean the leeks thoroughly. Chop the vegetables and simmer in the chicken stock for 35–40 minutes. Add the sliced mushrooms toward the end of the cooking time. Purée, leave to cool, then blend with the cream and season well. Top with cream and chopped chives.
To vary: Omit the mushrooms.

TERRINE EN CROUTE

1 roasting chicken, about 3½ lb. when trussed ·
the chicken giblets · 2 cups water · 1 onion ·
bouquet garni · seasoning · 2 slices bacon ·
½ lb. lean pork or veal · ½ lb. pork sausagemeat ·
1–2 tablespoons chopped parsley ·
For the pastry: ½ cup fat, preferably shortening ·
10 tablespoons water · 3 cups flour · pinch salt ·
1 egg

Take all the meat from the chicken; take care when removing the breast meat, for this must be cut into neat slices. Put the chicken bones, giblets, water, onion and herbs into a pan. Season, cover the pan and simmer for 30 minutes. Remove the lid, allow the liquid to boil rapidly to give 5 *tablespoons* really strong stock. Remove the liver. Grind the liver, the dark meat from the chicken legs and back (leave just the breast meat) and the bacon, pork or veal. Season and mix with 2½ tablepoons of the stock and the sausagemeat. Slice the chicken breast, put on a dish with the remaining stock and chopped parsley, season. Make the pastry by heating the fat in the water until melted. Add to the sifted flour and salt, knead well. Roll out, use three-quarters of the pastry to line a 2 lb. loaf pan. Fill this with alternate layers of ground chicken and sliced breast; begin and end with ground chicken. Roll out the remaining pastry to form a 'lid'. Damp the edges of the pastry, put on the 'lid' and flute the edges. Make a slit in the 'lid' and arrange 'leaves' of pastry on top. Brush with the beaten egg. Bake for 30 minutes in the center of a moderately hot to hot oven, 400–425°F, lower the heat to very moderate, 325°F, for a further 1 hour. Turn out and cool.

RASPBERRY PRINCESS

Make up a raspberry gelatin according to directions on the package. Pour over ½ cup crushed raspberries, then allow to cool and stiffen *very slightly*. Beat 3 egg whites stiffly. Gradually beat 1–2½ tablespoons sugar into the egg whites. Fold into the raspberry mixture. Spoon into glasses, decorate with raspberries and chill.

ALMOND SNAPS

2 large egg whites · 2–3 drops almond extract ·
½ cup sugar · ½ cup ground almonds

Grease 2–3 cookie trays with oil. Beat the egg whites stiffly, add the extract. Fold in the sugar and ground almonds. Divide the mixture into 18 balls. Put on the trays; allow space for them to spread out to about 3 inches in diameter. Flatten with your fingers. Bake for approximately 12 minutes just above the center of a moderate oven, 350–375°F. Bake one batch at a time. Remove from the oven, cool for 1 minute. Lift the first cookie from the trays, roll round the greased handle of a wooden spoon. Remove, put on a wire cooling tray. Repeat this process with remaining cookies.

Fruit Meringue Trifle

Mushroom Vichysoisse

Beat the eggs with the seasoning and water. Make 3–4 large omelets in the usual way, cooking these in the ½ cup butter. Fill with the lightly cooked vegetables tossed in the ¼ cup butter. Serve at once.

To vary: Use one vegetable only, such as tomatoes, instead of a mixture.

FRUIT MERINGUE TRIFLE

**1¼–1½ lb. dessert fruit★ · sugar to taste ·
2 cups heavy cream · up to ½ cup white wine ·
about 8 medium-sized meringue shells**

★*The picture shows raspberries, but sliced fresh peaches, apricots, pears, or a mixture of fruit may be used. Add a little white wine (extra to the ½ cup in the ingredients) or lemon juice to peaches, apricots or pears to prevent their discoloring. White wine can also be added to the berry fruit.*

Prepare the fruit, put into a bowl and sprinkle with sugar. Whip the cream until it holds its shape; put a little on one side for decoration. Gradually blend up to ½ cup white wine with the remaining cream. Sweeten to taste. Break the meringue shells (home-made or bought) into fairly large pieces. Put a layer at the bottom of a dish. Add half the fruit, then the cream and wine, then nearly all the remaining fruit (save a little for decoration). Top with meringue pieces, piped cream and fruit. This must be served within an hour of preparation so the meringue pieces keep crisp.

MENU

**SALAMI HORS D'OEUVRE
SUMMER OMELETS
WITH PEAS AND
NEW POTATOES
FRUIT MERINGUE TRIFLE**
This menu serves 6–8

SALAMI HORS D'OEUVRE

¾ lb. salami · 1 lettuce or other green salad ·
4 tomatoes · ¼ cucumber

Arrange slices of salami on a bed of lettuce or other green salad. Garnish with sliced tomatoes and cucumber. Serve with mustard or a mustard pickle.

SUMMER OMELETS

**Omelets: 12–16 eggs · seasoning ·
7½ tablespoons water · ½ cup butter ·
Filling: approximately 1 lb. cooked summer
vegetables · ¼ cup butter**

MENU

GOLDEN TOMATOES
PARCELED VEAL WITH
YOGURT AND SHERRY SAUCE
AND
MIXED SALAD OR SUMMER VEGETABLES
PEACH AND
STRAWBERRY BASKETS

GOLDEN TOMATOES

4 medium-sized tomatoes · 2 eggs ·
¼ lb. cream cheese ·
2½–4 tablespoons finely diced cucumber ·
seasoning · thick mayonnaise · sliced cucumber

Dip the tomatoes into boiling water for about 30 seconds, remove and cool. Take off the skins. Meanwhile, hard-cook the eggs. Shell, halve and put the yolks on one side. Chop the whites and put into a bowl. Add the cream cheese and diced cucumber. Cut a slice from the top of each tomato, scoop out the pulp, chop and add to the egg white mixture. Beat until fairly smooth. Season well. Spoon into the tomatoes, smooth flat on top, coat with thick mayonnaise and the chopped egg yolks. Serve on a bed of sliced cucumber.

PARCELED VEAL WITH YOGURT AND SHERRY SAUCE

3–4 slices fairly fat bacon · ¼ lb. mushrooms ·
1 tablespoon chopped parsley · 1 small onion ·
¼ cup butter or margarine · 1 cup fresh breadcrumbs ·
1 egg · seasoning · melted butter or oil ·
4 veal chops or fillets of veal ·
Sauce: 1¼ cups yogurt · little chopped parsley ·
seasoning · 2½ tablespoons sherry ·
2 teaspoons capers · 1 teaspoon prepared mustard ·
Garnish: lemon, parsley

Chop the bacon slices into narrow strips, slice the mushrooms and mix with the bacon. Add the chopped parsley, grated onion, butter or margarine, breadcrumbs, egg and seasoning. Stir well until the mixture binds. Cut 4 squares of foil, brush with melted butter or oil. Put a veal chop or fillet of veal in the center of each piece of foil. Spoon the stuffing on top and wrap the foil around the meat and stuffing to make a neat parcel. Lift into a meat pan and bake for approximately 30–35 minutes for thin fillets or 40–45 minutes for chops, towards the top of a hot oven, 425–450°F. To make the sauce, put the yogurt into a bowl over hot water, add the parsley, seasoning and sherry. Heat gently, then add the capers and mustard. Unwrap the 'parcels' carefully. Lift on to a dish, garnish with lemon and parsley and serve with the sauce.
To vary: Chicken pieces or fillets of fish could be cooked in the same way and would go well with the sauce.

PEACH AND STRAWBERRY BASKETS

4 peaches or 8 canned peach halves ·
¼ lb. strawberries · ½ cup heavy cream ·
1 tablespoon sieved confectioners' sugar ·
Topping: whole strawberries

Halve the peaches if using fresh fruit. Slice the strawberries;

do *not* mash. Blend with the whipped cream and sugar. Spread over the peach halves (cut side uppermost). If using fresh peaches make sure the cream mixture covers the cut surface to prevent discoloration. Top with whole strawberries. Decorate with strawberry leaves where possible.
To vary: Raspberries could be used in the same way as strawberries.

SOUR AND SWEET EGGS

4–6 eggs · 1 large onion · ¼ cup butter · ¼ cup flour ·
1¼ cups chicken stock or water and
chicken bouillon cube ·
2½ tablespoons brown malt vinegar ·
1¼ tablespoons honey · seasoning ·
2½ tablespoons diced gherkins

Hard-cook the eggs, crack and shell. Do not *over-cook* as they must be simmered for a short time in the sauce. Grate or chop the onion. Toss in the butter for a few minutes. Stir in the flour and cook over a low heat, then gradually add the chicken stock, or water and bouillon cube. Bring to the boil and cook until thickened. Add the vinegar, honey and seasoning. Put in the eggs and gherkins. Cover the pan and simmer for 2–3 minutes.

SALAMI AND POTATO SALAD

1 lb. cooked new potatoes, diced ·
few cooked green beans · few radishes, sliced ·
piece cucumber, sliced ·
2–3 sticks celery, chopped · 3–4 scallions, chopped ·
little mayonnaise · lettuce ·
¾–1 lb. sliced salami or other sausage

Mix the potatoes with the beans, radishes, cucumber, celery, scallions and mayonnaise to bind. Pile in the center of a bed of lettuce. Arrange the sliced salami or other sausage round the edge of the dish.
To vary: If preferred the lettuce can be served separately.

ORANGE CHERRY CREAMS

4 very large or 6 medium-sized oranges ·
1 package orange gelatin · ½ cup heavy cream ·
little sugar (optional) · fresh or canned cherries

Cut a slice from the top of each orange. Remove the pulp very carefully with a spoon. Drain the pulp, putting the juice into a measure and the pieces of pulp on one side. Remove any seeds and skin from the pulp. Add enough hot water to the orange juice to give 2 cups liquid. Dissolve the orange gelatin in this. Allow to cool and begin to stiffen then beat with the lightly whipped cream. Taste and add a little sugar if wished. Put the orange pulp and a few pitted ripe or canned cherries at the bottom of each orange case. Spoon the orange cream over the fruit. Decorate with cherries.

Salami and Potato Salad

Balanced Menus for Beauty

One cannot plan a sensible beauty routine without considering the value of various foods and their effect upon good health and beauty.
The menus that follow are designed to give interesting and appetizing meals planned around the many foods that contribute to a nutritious diet.
The footnote after each menu indicates why I have chosen them. All menus in this chapter serve 4 unless stated otherwise.

MENU

HERRING HORS D'OEUVRE
CHEESE AND ONION HOT-POT
WITH ENDIVE COLESLAW
FRESH FRUIT
This menu serves 4–6

HERRING HORS D'OEUVRE

4 medium-sized herrings or mackerel · seasoning ·
little oil · 1 small onion · 1 dessert apple ·
little sherry · mayonnaise · curry powder ·
½–1½ tablespoons tomato paste ·
2½–4 tablespoons plain yogurt · 1 raw carrot ·
1 teaspoon grated raw onion · 1 hard-cooked egg ·
lettuce and watercress ·
Garnish: lemon twists

Fillet the herrings. Season, brush with a little oil and broil carefully so the flesh does not break – *do not over-cook*. Cool, then cut into neat pieces. Blend 1 herring with the finely chopped onion, finely chopped apple and a little sherry. Blend the second herring with mayonnaise flavored with curry powder. Mix the tomato paste with the yogurt and toss the third herring in this mixture. Mix the last herring with the grated carrot, onion and chopped hard-cooked egg. Arrange the four mixtures on a bed of lettuce and watercress. Garnish with lemon twists.

CHEESE AND ONION HOT-POT

1 lb. potatoes · 1 lb. onions · ½ lb. Cheddar cheese ·
seasoning · little melted margarine ·
10 tablespoons milk

Peel and slice the potatoes and onions very thinly. Slice or grate the cheese. Put layers of the potato, cheese and onion into a casserole, seasoning each layer and brushing with a little melted margarine. Begin and end with potatoes. Pour the milk over the mixture. Bake in the center of a very moderate oven, 325–350°F, for about 1¼ hours.

ENDIVE COLESLAW

1 small cabbage · 1 carrot · 3–4 heads of endive ·
4 tablespoons plain yogurt ·
1–2 teaspoons prepared mustard ·
squeeze lemon juice · chopped parsley

Shred the heart of the cabbage finely, mix with the grated carrot and the chopped base of the heads of endive. Blend the yogurt with the mustard and lemon juice. Toss the vegetables in this. Put into a shallow dish, top with chopped parsley and arrange the tips of endive around the dish.

Analysis
Herring is an excellent source of protein, fat (for creating a feeling of warmth), and Vitamin A which also helps to give a good skin and healthy eyes. Although potatoes are a 'starchy' vegetable, which must be omitted in a very stringent slimming diet, they *do* contain Vitamin C and like all starches (eaten in sensible amounts) provide energy. Cheese gives calcium for strong teeth, bones and nails, as well as protein. This meal has plenty of raw vegetables for roughage.

MENU

GRAPEFRUIT
OMELET FILLED WITH
COTTAGE CHEESE AND
CHOPPED CHIVES
SPINACH

Analysis
This is a perfectly satisfying low calorie meal. If you find unsweetened grapefruit too acid, moisten with liquid sugar substitute blended with hot water. Cottage cheese, blended with plenty of chives for additional flavor, makes an excellent filling for an omelet. Cook the omelet lightly, so it is pleasantly moist.

Herring Hors d'Oeuvre, Cheese and Onion Hot-Pot with Endive Coleslaw

MENU

**AVOCADO SOUFFLÉ
COLD BEEF WITH
BAKED POTATOES AND
MIXED SALADS
APRICOT FOOL**

AVOCADO SOUFFLÉ

**2 small (or 1 large) ripe avocados ·
juice 1 small lemon · 2 teaspoons olive oil ·
seasoning · 3 eggs**

Halve the avocados, remove the pits and scoop the pulp from the skins. Mash with the lemon juice, olive oil and seasoning. Separate the egg yolks from the whites. Add the yolks and beat well. Fold in the stiffly beaten egg whites. Put into a buttered or oiled 1 quart soufflé dish and bake for 20–25 minutes in the center of a moderate oven, 350–375°F. Do not over-cook as this soufflé is best not too set.
To vary: Put a layer of shrimp or crabmeat at the bottom of the dish.

Apricot Fool

APRICOT FOOL

**½ lb. dried apricots · 1¼ cups water · juice 1 lemon ·
sugar or sugar substitute to taste ·
½ cup heavy cream, thick custard or yogurt ·
Topping: slivered browned almonds**

Soak the apricots in the water and lemon juice for 12–24 hours. Simmer until tender. Purée and sweeten with sugar or sugar substitute. Blend with the whipped cream, custard or yogurt. Spoon into 4 glasses and top with slivered browned almonds.
To vary: The fool can be topped with a spoonful of fresh cream or yogurt instead of, or as well as, the almonds.

*Citrus Fruit Cocktails, Broiled Sole and Cauliflower Niçoise,
Gingerbread with Apple Sauce*

Analysis

Avocados are an unusual fruit for they are rich in protein, so the first course of this meal is equally suitable for a light meal. Try to have potatoes cooked in their skin as often as possible, as they give extra flavor, roughage and Vitamin C. Fresh vegetable salads provide plenty of Vitamin C and are low in calories. Dried apricots are an excellent source of iron.

MENU

**CITRUS FRUIT COCKTAILS
BROILED SOLE AND
CAULIFLOWER NIÇOISE
GINGERBREAD
WITH APPLE SAUCE**

CITRUS FRUIT COCKTAILS

**1 large grapefruit · juice ½ or 1 small lemon ·
juice 3–4 large oranges ·
sugar, sugar substitute or honey ·
few bruised mint leaves (if available)**

Squeeze the juice from the grapefruit, mix with the lemon and orange juice. Add a little sugar, sugar substitute or honey to sweeten and a few bruised mint leaves when available. Serve in glasses.

BROILED SOLE

**4 large (or 8 small) fillets of sole · little milk · butter ·
Garnish: parsley, lemons**

Soak the fish in a little milk for 30 minutes. Drain, brush with butter and broil. Garnish with parsley and quartered lemons.

CAULIFLOWER NIÇOISE

**1 medium-sized cauliflower · seasoning · 2 onions ·
¼ cup margarine · 4 large tomatoes ·
1 teaspoon cornstarch ·
1 tablespoon chopped gherkins**

Cook the cauliflower in boiling salted water. Meanwhile, chop the onions, and fry in the margarine. Add the peeled chopped tomatoes, cook until a thick purée. Blend ½ cup cauliflower water with the cornstarch, add to the tomato mixture with the gherkins and seasoning. Cook until thickened and spoon over the cauliflower.

GINGERBREAD WITH APPLE SAUCE

Make the gingerbread as page 68. Cut enough portions for 4, warm in the oven and top with apple sauce (see page 54).

Analysis

Fresh citrus fruits are an excellent start to any meal. They ensure an adequate amount of Vitamin C, which is needed daily and cannot be stored in the body. Fish is a low-calorie source of protein, and broiling the most digestible method of cooking. All too often vegetable liquid is not used and this retains valuable mineral salts, so the sauce gives added nutrients as well as interest and flavor to the meal. Black molasses is used rarely, except in gingerbreads, but it is one of the best sources of iron.

MENU

CHICKEN LIVER SCRAMBLE
COTTAGE CHEESE AND NUT SALAD
YOGURT CALIFORNIA

CHICKEN LIVER SCRAMBLE

4 chicken livers · ¼ cup butter · seasoning · 4 eggs · wholewheat toast

Chop the chicken livers finely. Heat in the butter, add the well-seasoned eggs and scramble lightly. Serve on or with crisp wholewheat toast.

Yogurt California

COTTAGE CHEESE AND NUT SALAD

1 tablespoon chopped parsley and/or mint · ¾ lb. cottage cheese · lettuce and/or other salad greens · salted or plain peanuts or cashew nuts · 8 apple rings · mayonnaise

Blend the chopped parsley and/or mint with the cottage cheese. Pile on to a bed of greens, top with the peanuts or cashew nuts. Arrange the apple rings, dipped in mayonnaise and topped with more nuts, around the cottage cheese. Serve a dish of sliced, well-seasoned tomatoes and cucumber separately.

YOGURT CALIFORNIA

½ lb. prunes · cold water · little grated orange rind · little fresh orange juice · yogurt · little honey (optional)

Cover the prunes with cold water, add the orange rind and juice. Leave to soak overnight, then simmer until tender, unless using tenderized prunes which will become quite soft with soaking alone. Chill and serve with yogurt. Add a little honey to the prunes for a sweet flavor.

Analysis
Wholewheat bread gives valuable Vitamin B and mineral salts. Liver, eggs and prunes are all excellent sources of iron, a mineral that is often neglected in modern diets. The cheese, with nuts, liver and eggs, ensures plenty of protein in this meal and cottage cheese, like all cheese, is an excellent source of calcium, while being low in calories. Fresh tomatoes give Vitamin C and yogurt is one of the easiest and most nutritious desserts. Encourage all the family to eat yogurt.

MENU

SHRIMP AND GRAPEFRUIT COCKTAIL
ALPINE EGGS WITH CREAMED SPINACH
MELON

SHRIMP AND GRAPEFRUIT COCKTAIL

2 grapefruit · ¼ lb. shrimp · mayonnaise or seasoned yogurt · lettuce

Halve the grapefruit, remove the segments and blend with the shrimp. Toss in mayonnaise or seasoned yogurt. Put a layer of finely shredded lettuce into each grapefruit 'shell' or into glasses. Top with the shrimp and grapefruit mixture.
To vary: Use sliced avocado in place of the grapefruit, and add a few drops of chili sauce.

ALPINE EGGS

4 thin slices wholewheat or brown bread · 2 tablespoons butter · ¼ lb. cottage or cream cheese · little finely chopped onion or chives · 4 eggs · salt · celery salt · cayenne pepper · white pepper

Put the bread into a long, shallow, oven-proof dish. Spread with butter, cover with cheese and a sprinkling of onion or chives. Heat for 10 minutes above the center of a moderately hot oven, 375–400°F. Separate the eggs, put the whites into a bowl. Pour the egg yolks carefully into the center of each slice of bread. Beat the egg whites until very stiff, add seasonings. Pile the meringue mixture around the egg yolks so the bread and cheese is covered. Return to the oven for 15 minutes, lower the heat to very moderate, 325°F (this gives time to eat the first course).

Analysis
Shell fish is a low-calorie protein and combines with fresh grapefruit (which gives Vitamin C) for an interesting hors d'oeuvre. Eggs and cheese are as nutritious as meat or fish for a main dish and bread also provides protein. Spinach is rich in iron. Melon has no real vitamin value but is low in calories and very refreshing.

Shrimp and Grapefruit Cocktail

Celebration Menus

Something to celebrate often means a special meal. It may be the start of a new job or a new school, a celebration dinner party for an anniversary, or a birthday party. The menus on the next pages give ideas for several different types of celebration meals — from formal dinner or luncheon parties, buffet parties of all kinds to informal wine and cheese parties.

Lobster Soufflé, Veal Chops with Chestnut Purée, Savory Scalloped Potatoes, Peas French Style, Pear and Chocolate Gâteau

A special dinner or luncheon menu which would be easy to prepare and serve. Quantities are for 6 people.

Advance Preparations: Prepare the fresh lobster stock.

Make the thick sauce in the pan for the soufflé and the thin sauce for the accompaniment, cover both with damp paper. You can blend the pouring sauce in a blender before transferring to the double boiler (see recipe) to make sure it is very smooth. Prepare the cutlets and chestnut purée. Cut the potatoes, shell the peas; keep both potatoes and peas in cold water. Peel and slice the onions. Make the gâteau, fill and store in a cool place. Arrange the cheese tray.

LOBSTER SOUFFLÉ

1 small lobster · 1¼ cups water · seasoning ·
3 tablespoons butter · ¼ cup flour ·
3 tablespoons heavy cream · 5 eggs · seasoning ·
Sauce: 2 tablespoons butter · ¼ cup flour ·
1¼ cups milk · pinch anchovy extract (optional) ·
about 5 tablespoons heavy cream

Brandy Soufflé

Remove the lobster meat from the shell. Put the shell into a pan, add the water and seasoning. Cover the pan and simmer for 15 minutes. Measure the stock, put 10 tablespoons on one side for the soufflé and simmer the rest until it is reduced to 2½ tablespoons only for the sauce. Heat the butter in a large pan, stir in the flour and cook for several minutes. Gradually blend in the lobster stock. Bring to the boil, stirring well, and cook until a thick sauce. Draw to one side, then add the heavy cream and most of the flaked lobster meat; save the neatest pieces to go into the sauce. Separate the eggs, add the yolks and seasoning, and lastly fold in the stiffly beaten egg whites. Put into a buttered 1½–2 quart 8-inch soufflé dish and bake for approximately 35 minutes in the center of a moderate oven, 350–375°F, until risen and firm. Serve with the sauce.

To make the sauce, heat the butter in a pan. Stir in the flour and cook for several minutes. Gradually blend in the milk and the 2½ tablespoons lobster stock. Bring to the boil, stir well and cook until thickened. Add the anchovy extract. Transfer to the top of a double boiler over hot water and cover with very damp waxed paper. Add the cream, any extra seasoning required and the tiny pieces of chopped lobster just before serving.

CUTLETS OF VEAL OR VENISON WITH CHESTNUT PURÉE

6 large or 12 medium-sized veal or venison cutlets or chops · butter ·
Marinade: 2½ tablespoons olive oil ·
2½ tablespoons white wine vinegar or white wine ·
1 clove garlic · seasoning · little chopped parsley ·
Garnish: sliced tomatoes and/or lemon and parsley

Put the cutlets into a marinade made with oil and vinegar or white wine (you can use red wine vinegar or red wine for venison if wished), the crushed clove of garlic, seasoning and parsley. Turn the cutlets and leave for several hours. This tenderizes the meat and counteracts the very dry texture of these particular meats. Lift the cutlets from the marinade, but do not drain. Put into an oven-proof dish, top with a very little butter and cover with foil. Bake for about 40 minutes – 1 hour, depending on the size, towards the top of the oven.

Serve with chestnut purée (see below) and garnish with sliced tomatoes and/or lemon and parsley.

To make the chestnut purée, simply heat canned chestnut purée with enough brown stock to make a soft consistency. Season very well and keep hot in an attractive serving dish.

SAVORY SCALLOPED POTATOES

Follow the recipe variation on page 60 but use 1½ lb. potatoes and 2 sliced onions.

PEAS FRENCH STYLE

1 lettuce · about 1¼ lb. fresh shelled or frozen peas ·
2 tablespoons butter · seasoning · few scallions ·
about 2½ tablespoons water

Line an attractive casserole with very damp lettuce leaves. Add the peas, butter, seasoning and chopped scallions. Cover with the water and very damp lettuce leaves. Wrap the *outside* of the dish with foil, so the lettuce does not scorch, and cook on the same shelf as the potatoes for about 1 hour. To serve, just remove the top layer of lettuce. Do not strain the peas; the little liquid in the dish is delicious.

PEAR AND CHOCOLATE GÂTEAU

1 cup margarine or butter · 1 cup sugar ·
4 large eggs ·
1½ cups self-rising flour or all-purpose flour and 1½ teaspoons baking powder · ¼ cup cocoa ·
¼ cup ground almonds ·
1–2½ tablespoons warm water ·
1 large can pear halves · 1½ cups heavy cream ·
little brandy ·
Decoration: browned slivered almonds

Cream the margarine or butter with the sugar until soft and light. Gradually beat in the eggs. Sift together the flour (or flour and baking powder) and cocoa. Add the ground almonds and fold into the creamed mixture. Add 1 tablespoon warm water to give a soft consistency, or about 2 tablespoons if the eggs are only medium-sized. Divide the mixture between

Sole Normandie

two greased and lined 9-inch cake pans and bake just above the center of a moderate oven, 350–375°F, for approximately 25–30 minutes, until just firm to the touch. Turn out very carefully. Allow to cool. Drain the pears well. Whip the cream, flavor with a little brandy. Spread some of the cream over one of the cakes, top with sliced pears and the second cake. Spread some of the remaining cream over the cake. Decorate with pear slices, browned slivered almonds and piped cream.

To vary: If wished, the sides of the cake can be covered with browned almonds, as shown in the picture. First coat the sides in cream and then roll in the almonds.

Suggested Wines
Serve a well chilled Chablis or other dry white wine with the soufflé and a claret with the main course.

MENU

**PÂTÉ WITH TOAST AND BUTTER
SOLE NORMANDIE
NEW POTATOES
GREEN PEAS
BRANDY SOUFFLÉ
CHEESE TRAY**

A luxurious but fairly light dinner menu for 4–6 people.

Advance Preparations: Make the pâté at least 24 hours beforehand; it also freezes well for up to 6 weeks. Prepare all the ingredients for the Sole Normandie or prepare the complete recipe and put into an oven-proof serving dish, in which case take particular care that the sole is not over-cooked, and make the sauce a little thinner than usual (add 3¾ tablespoons extra milk or cream). This allows for evaporation when reheating the dish. Prepare the sauce for the soufflé, cover with damp paper and prepare the soufflé dish with the Lady fingers and cherries. Arrange the cheese tray.

CREAMED LIVER PÂTÉ

½ lb. calf's liver · ½ lb. pig's liver · ½ lb. bacon ·
1–2 cloves garlic · 1 small onion · ½ cup butter ·
¼ cup flour · 10 tablespoons milk ·
½ teaspoon finely chopped mixed fresh herbs ·
2½ tablespoons heavy cream · 2½ tablespoons brandy ·
seasoning

Grind the liver, bacon, garlic and onion. Heat ¼ cup of butter in a pan, stir in the flour and cook for several minutes, then add the milk. Stir over a medium heat until a thick sauce. Add the liver mixture and the remaining ingredients, except the butter, and blend thoroughly. Butter an oven-proof dish and put in the mixture. Cover with well-buttered foil or waxed paper. Stand the dish in a bain-marie (container of cold water) and cook for 1¼ hours in the center of a slow to very moderate oven, 300–325°F. Take the pâté out of the oven and put a light weight over the top; this makes it easier to slice. Melt the remaining butter and pour over the top of the cold pâté. Serve with lettuce and wedges of lemon. This would serve 8–10, so there will be some left.

SOLE NORMANDIE
This is a wonderful combination of white and shell fish. Other white fish can be used instead.

1 pint mussels · ½ cup water · *bouquet garni* · seasoning ·
1 cup shrimp · few oysters · 1 onion or shallot ·
10 tablespoons white wine · 8 fillets sole ·
6 tablespoons butter · ½ cup flour ·
10 tablespoons milk · 10 tablespoons heavy cream ·
¼ lb. button mushrooms

Wash the mussels, scrub well, and remove any 'beard' or weed attached to the shell. Discard any that do not close when sharply tapped as this means the mussel is dead and could therefore be 'off'. Put into a pan with the water, *bouquet garni* and seasoning. Heat until the mussels open. Lift the mussels out of the liquid. Shell the shrimp and open the oysters. Add the shrimp shells, the liquid from the oyster shells, the chopped onion or shallot and wine to the mussel liquid. Simmer for 15 minutes. Strain carefully and return to the pan. Put the fillets of sole into this; either fold or keep whole if the pan is sufficiently large. Simmer until *just* tender. Lift the sole out of the liquid. Arrange on a flat dish or in individual dishes and keep warm. Meanwhile, make a coating sauce with 4 tablespoons butter, the flour, milk, cream and strained fish liquid. Stir well until smooth. Fry the sliced mushrooms in the remaining butter. Add to the sauce with the shell fish, warm for 1–2 minutes only (so the shell fish does not toughen). Spoon over the fish.

BRANDY SOUFFLÉ

about 12 Lady fingers ·
7½ tablespoons brandy (or Curaçao) ·
¼ lb. chopped glacé cherries★ · 2 tablespoons butter ·
¼ cup flour · 10 tablespoons milk ·
10 tablespoons light cream · ¼ cup sugar ·
3 egg yolks · 4 egg whites
★or use a mixture of candied fruits

Arrange the Lady fingers in the bottom of a soufflé dish, add 3½ tablespoons brandy and the chopped cherries or fruit. Heat the butter in a large pan. Stir in the flour and cook gently for several minutes. Gradually stir in the milk and cream. Bring slowly to the boil, stirring all the time, and cook until thickened. Add the sugar, remaining brandy and the egg yolks. Fold in the stiffly beaten egg whites. Pile over the Lady fingers. Bake for approximately 40 minutes in the center of a moderate oven, 350–375°F. Serve at once.

Suggested Wines
A rosé or champagne would be a perfect accompaniment to this menu. Both should be served well chilled.

```
MENU

LOBSTER THERMIDOR
CHICKEN HAWAIIAN SALAD
WITH NEW POTATOES
HOT MELON AND GINGER
```

This is an ideal hot weather luncheon or dinner menu which is easy to prepare. Quantities serve up to 8 people but the lobster serves 4 as a main dish.

Advance Preparations: Make the sauce for the lobster dish, but do not finish cooking until the last minute. Prepare the ingredients for the salad, do not mix until just before the meal. Prepare the melon and keep in a covered container so it does not dry out. Prepare the sauce and heat at the last minute.

LOBSTER THERMIDOR
This is one of the classic lobster dishes.

2 medium-sized lobsters · few drops olive oil ·
¼ cup butter · 1 small onion or shallot · ¼ cup flour ·
1¼ cups milk · 1 teaspoon chopped chervil ·
½ teaspoon chopped tarragon ·
1 teaspoon chopped parsley · seasoning ·
1–2 teaspoons French or English mustard ·
7½ tablespoons white wine ·
3½ tablespoons heavy cream ·
2½–4 tablespoons grated Parmesan cheese ·
Garnish: lemons, parsley

Split the lobsters, remove the intestinal vein and discard. Take the flesh from the shells and put on one side. Polish the shells with 2 or 3 drops of olive oil. Remove the flesh from the claws. Heat the butter, fry the finely chopped onion or shallot. Stir in the flour and cook for several minutes, stirring all the time. Gradually blend in the milk, bring to the boil and cook until thickened. Stir well to keep the sauce smooth. Lower the heat, add the herbs and seasoning. This dish *should* have a definite flavor of mustard, but add this gradually to suit your own taste. Add the wine and cream to the sauce, and *simmer* very gently until a coating consistency again. Add the lobster flesh and heat for a few minutes only. *Do not over-cook.* Spoon into the lobster shells. Top with cheese and brown under the broiler. Serve garnished with lemons and parsley.
To vary: Use large shrimp instead of lobster; serve in an attractive oven-proof dish.
Use 2 large crabs in place of the lobster and serve in the well-scrubbed crab shells, or in an oven-proof serving dish.

CHICKEN HAWAIIAN SALAD

1 cup almonds ·
1 cooked roasting chicken, about 2–2½ lb. trussed ·
1 fresh pineapple · 1 green pepper ·
1 head endive or few sticks celery · mayonnaise ·
lettuce ·
Garnish: tomatoes, cucumber or extra endive

Blanch the almonds and brown the nuts under the broiler or in the oven. Dice the cooked chicken. Cut the top off the pineapple (keep this if the leaves are pleasantly green). Cut pineapple into rings, cut away the skin and core. Do this over a bowl so the juice is not wasted. Dice the pineapple. Blend most of the almonds, the chicken, pineapple, diced green pepper (discard the core and seeds) and the chopped endive or celery. Blend the required amount of mayonnaise with any pineapple juice. Toss the chicken mixture in this. Pile on to a bed of lettuce, sprinkle with the remaining almonds. Garnish with quartered tomatoes and sliced cucumber or endive leaves. Top the salad with the pineapple leaves if retained.
To vary: Use 2 large oranges in place of the pineapple. Remove all the skin, pith and seeds.

HOT MELON AND GINGER
This is an excellent way to serve the less luxurious melons which often have relatively little flavor.

1 ripe but firm melon · juice of 1 lemon ·
½ cup water · ¼ cup sugar ·
2½–4 tablespoons preserved or crystallized ginger

Either slice or halve the melon and remove the seeds, then dice the flesh or cut into balls (with vegetable scoop). Heat the lemon juice, water and sugar and the diced ginger. Add the melon and heat for a few minutes only. Spoon into glasses. Serve with cream or ice cream.
To vary: Use 2½ tablespoons ginger syrup from preserved ginger and heat with the lemon juice.

Suggested Wines
Choose a white wine for the first course – a Pouilly Fuisse or Pouilly Fume would be ideal. You can continue to serve this with the chicken salad, but a rosé or sparkling Burgundy would be very pleasant. All should be served well chilled.

Chicken Hawaiian Salad

MENU

CHICKEN À LA KIEV WITH GREEN SALAD
AND CREAMED OR NEW POTATOES
ICED CHRISTMAS PUDDING
CHEESE TRAY

This is a good choice for a luncheon menu or for an after-theater supper. It serves 4 people. It is better not to have an hors d'oeuvre if you are responsible for the cooking, so you can give your undivided attention to the chicken dish.

Advance Preparations: Prepare the chicken dish completely ready for frying. Make the salad. The ice cream can be made and frozen several days beforehand or even longer if wished. Arrange the cheese tray.

Iced Christmas Pudding

CHICKEN À LA KIEV

This classic chicken dish is deliciously simple, except the chicken must be cooked in deep fat or oil until crisp. This is troublesome if you are entertaining. I have experimented by frying the chicken for about 5 minutes until very crisp on the outside, draining this, then putting it on a baking tray to cook for 25–30 minutes in a hot oven. If you want a slight variation on the usual recipe, blend the butter filling with a little finely chopped red and green pepper, chives and chopped rosemary or thyme. Finely chopped mushrooms can also be added to the butter with a good squeeze of lemon juice.

**4 small young spring chickens · ½ cup butter ·
Coating: 2 eggs · ¾ cup dry breadcrumbs ·
To fry: olive oil or well clarified fat**

Ingredients for Chicken à la Kiev

Bone the chicken (or ask the butcher to do this for you). In order to bone the chicken easily do check you have a very well sharpened and flexible knife, for this is essential if you are not to break the delicate flesh. Work slowly so you 'ease' the flesh away from the bones; you should finish with all the chicken flesh intact and free from bones.

Put the bird with the neck towards you. Loosen the skin away from the flesh at the neck end of the bird and gradually work your finger (better than a knife) under the skin over the breasts – do not tear the skin, simply loosen it away from the flesh. Cut away the wishbone with the knife. Turn the bird so the breast is on the chopping board.

Cut the shoulder bones from the flesh of the bird and sever these from the body. Cut off the wing tips and discard; then ease the flesh from the wing bones. Ease the skin away from the flesh of the thighs, then gradually cut the flesh from the thigh bones and the drumsticks. Some people leave the very end piece of the drumsticks (where it joins the foot) as this gives a more interesting shape to the bird but this is not necessary with this recipe. Work slowly and carefully and cut away the breast bone, back bone and the parson's nose.

Spread the chickens out flat. Put a quarter of the butter on each chicken, roll firmly. Coat with beaten egg and crumbs. Fry in hot oil or fat for 12–15 minutes until golden brown and tender. Drain on absorbent paper, serve at once. Pierce each chicken *gently* before eating so the butter does not spurt out too violently.

To vary: Instead of using a small spring chicken, use the breast of an ordinary chicken. Bone out the breast, then fill with the butter and continue as above.

ICED CHRISTMAS PUDDING

This ice cream can be served throughout the year, but the mixture of fruits makes it ideal at Christmas time. Freeze the ice cream as quickly as possible in a home freezer or in the ice-making compartment of a refrigerator. The refrigerator should be turned to the coldest setting 1 hour before the ice cream is made.

**10 tablespoons milk · ¼ lb. marshmallows ·
1 teaspoon cocoa · 1 teaspoon instant coffee ·
½ cup raisins · ¼ cup white raisins · ¼ cup currants ·
2½ tablespoons sherry · 2¼ cups Maraschino cherries ·
½ cup chopped nuts · 1¼ cups heavy cream ·
Decoration (optional): Maraschino cherries**

Put the milk, marshmallows, cocoa and coffee in a pan. Heat gently until the marshmallows are nearly melted. Allow to cool. Meanwhile, mix the dried fruit with the sherry. Allow to stand for 30 minutes then add to the marshmallow mixture with the diced cherries and nuts. Freeze for a short time until slightly thickened. Fold the whipped cream into this mixture and pack into a chilled bowl. Freeze until firm. Turn out, decorate with cherries if liked, and serve with more whipped cream (flavored with brandy and sweetened with confectioners' sugar). This ice cream can also be served with brandy butter.

To vary: Use 2½ tablespoons brandy or kirsch in place of the sherry.

Suggested Wines

If serving this dish for luncheon, a white Rhine wine would be an ideal accompaniment.

If serving for an after-theater supper, you may prefer champagne or a sparkling Burgundy.

Carpet Bag Steaks

MENU

**SMOKED SALMON
WITH SCRAMBLED EGGS
BROWN BREAD AND BUTTER
CARPET BAG STEAKS
FRIED POTATOES/GREEN BEANS
OR PEAS
GREEN SALAD
BRIGADE PUDDING WITH CREAM**

This is a celebration menu for people who like 'good plain food', with a new twist. It is a very satisfying meal – ideal for hungry men – and serves 6 people.

Advance Preparations: Make the pudding. Fill the steaks. Arrange the smoked salmon on individual plates and cover; scramble the eggs at the last minute and put beside the smoked salmon.

CARPET BAG STEAKS

6 *thick* pieces of fillet ·
about 24 prepared mussels or 6–12 oysters ·
½ cup butter · 3 teaspoons chopped parsley ·
lemon juice · seasoning ·
Garnish: cooked tomatoes, mushrooms, parsley

Split the steak to make 'pockets'. Mix the mussels or sliced oysters with ¼ cup melted butter, the chopped parsley, a squeeze of lemon juice and seasoning. Put into the steak 'pockets'. Skewer firmly or sew with fine string or thread. Brush the steaks with remaining melted butter and broil to personal taste until tender. Remove the skewers, string or thread and serve with tomatoes, mushrooms and parsley.

BRIGADE PUDDING

Suet crust pastry: 2 cups self-rising flour
or all-purpose flour with 2 teaspoons baking powder
pinch of salt · ½ cup chopped or shredded suet or
butter or margarine · water to mix ·

Brigade Pudding

Filling: 2½ tablespoons corn syrup · ½ lb. mincemeat · 3 large cooking apples

Sift the flour or flour and baking powder and salt together. Add the suet or rub in the butter or margarine and bind with water to a rolling consistency. Roll out very thinly. Cut into 4 rounds – one the size of the base of a 1½ quart bowl, one a little bigger, the next a little bigger, and finally one almost as large as the top of the bowl. Put the corn syrup into the greased bowl, add the first round of pastry, then one-third of the mincemeat blended with the peeled grated apples, the next round of pastry, then mincemeat and apple, then the third round, then mincemeat and apple. Top with the final round of pastry. Cover the bowl with waxed paper and foil. Steam over boiling water for 2½ hours. Turn out and serve with cream or custard sauce.

Suggested Wines
A well-chilled white wine can be served with the smoked salmon and a claret (Margaux, St. Emilion) or a red Burgundy (Beaune, Beaujolais) with the steak.

MENU

SALMON WALEWSKA
WITH MIXED SALAD
ALMOND MERINGUE DESSERT
FROSTED CAMEMBERT CHEESE
AND CHEESE STRAWS (see page 118)

This menu can be served for a formal meal or as a buffet meal. It serves 8 people.

Advance Preparations: Prepare the fish and sauce and cook at the last minute. Make the dessert and put the Camembert cheese into the freezing compartment of the refrigerator or freezer for 30 minutes. The cheese straws can be made some days beforehand and stored in an airtight tin. They can also be deep-frozen but are best if they are then warmed through before serving.

SALMON WALEWSKA

Although salmon is the ideal fish for this dish, it is almost as delicious with cutlets or fillets of white fish, such as halibut, turbot or tuna. Lobster is the shell fish which is traditionally added to the sauce, but others such as crab or shrimp could be used.

8 salmon steaks · 1 cup butter ·
3½ tablespoons lemon juice · seasoning · 6 egg yolks ·
2 small or 1 large lobster ·
Garnish: lemon, cucumber, lobster claws

Brush the salmon with ¼ cup melted butter. Sprinkle with ½ tablespoon lemon juice and season lightly. Put into an oven-proof dish, cover with foil, and bake for 20–25 minutes in the center of a moderate oven, 350–375°F, until just tender – do *not* over-cook.
Put the egg yolks, a little seasoning and remaining lemon juice into a bowl over a pan of hot, but not boiling, water and beat until thick. Gradually beat in the remaining butter then add the diced pieces of lobster. Keep warm but do not over-heat otherwise the sauce will curdle. Lift the salmon on to a platter, top with the sauce and garnish with the lemon, cucumber and lobster claws.

ALMOND MERINGUE DESSERT

Meringue: 6 egg whites · 1½ cups sugar ·
¼ cup slivered blanched almonds ·
Filling: 1 lb. fresh chestnuts plus few drops vanilla extract, or use 1 can (approximately 16¾ oz.) *unsweetened* chestnut purée · ¼ cup butter ·
½ cup sifted confectioners' sugar (optional) ·
1¼ cups heavy cream ·
2 tablespoons slivered blanched almonds

Cut out three rounds, approximately 7–8 inches in diameter, of waxed paper. Oil each round *very lightly* and put on to flat cookie trays. Beat the egg whites until *very* stiff then gradually beat in half the sugar. Fold in nearly all the remaining sugar. Pipe or spread the meringue over the oiled waxed paper to give neat rounds. Sprinkle with the almonds and remaining sugar. Dry out the meringues for 2½–3 hours in a very slow oven, 225–250°F. Lift the meringue rounds off the trays while still warm. Carefully peel away the paper, then transfer to wire cooling trays. When cold store in an airtight tin, separating the rounds with waxed paper. The cooked meringue rounds can be stored in an airtight tin for several weeks.
To make the filling, slit the skins of the well-washed chestnuts and either simmer in water for nearly 10 minutes or roast in a hot oven for nearly 15 minutes. Remove both outer shells and brown skin while warm. Put the nuts into a pan with a little water and vanilla extract and simmer until tender, then purée. Blend the fresh or canned chestnut purée into the creamed butter and sugar, if using.
Whip the cream until firm enough to pipe. Spread the first round of meringue with half the chestnut purée, put on the second round and top with whipped cream. Add the third round of meringue, and top this with the rest of the chestnut purée. Decorate with a piped border of cream and the almonds. Serve soon after preparing so the meringue does not soften. Gives 8 large slices, but will serve 12.

Suggested Wines
A well chilled rosé is ideal for this menu.

> ## MENU
>
> MELON
> VEAL MORNAY
> NEW POATOES
> ASPARAGUS OR GREEN PEAS
> CHESTNUT AND RUM SWISS GÂTEAU
> (see page 112)
> CARAMELED GRAPES

A menu that is equally good for a lunch or dinner to serve 4.

Advance Preparations: Slice the melon, keep in a cool place. Fry the veal, make the sauce; reheat this very carefully to prevent over-cooking. Prepare the gâteau and the grapes.

VEAL MORNAY
Fried fillets of tender veal make an easy and delicious dish.

4 thin slices (fillets) of veal ·
4 small slices cooked ham · seasoning · little flour ·
1 egg · 2¼–4 tablespoons dry breadcrumbs ·
¼ cup butter · 1½ tablespoons olive oil ·
Sauce: 2 tablespoons butter · ¼ cup flour ·
10 tablespoons milk ·
10 tablespoons white wine (or use 1½ cups milk and omit wine) · 1 teaspoon French mustard ·
2½ tablespoons heavy cream ·
1 cup grated Cheddar or Gruyère cheese ·
Garnish: cooked small new potatoes, chopped parsley, lemon, cooked peas or asparagus tips

Flatten the veal with a rolling pin. Place the slices of ham so they cover half of each fillet then fold the meat to cover the ham. Dip in seasoned flour then in beaten egg and crumbs. Heat the butter and oil in a large pan and fry the veal quickly on either side until crisp and golden brown. Lower the heat and continue cooking until tender. Lift out of the pan, drain on absorbent paper. This is necessary as the veal is served with a rather rich cheese sauce. Heat the butter, stir in the flour and cook for several minutes. Gradually blend in the milk and stir until thickened, lower the heat and add the wine, mustard and seasoning. Stir the cream and cheese into the sauce just before serving. Do not allow the sauce to boil. Arrange the veal on a dish in a border of cooked small new potatoes, tossed with parsley. Put a spoonful of sauce in the center of each fillet, top with a twist of lemon and a few peas or asparagus tips. Serve the rest of the sauce separately.

CARAMELED GRAPES

¾ cup sugar · 7½ tablespoons water ·
small bunches grapes

Put the sugar into a saucepan with the water. Stir until the sugar has dissolved then boil steadily until a pale golden caramel. Dip small bunches of grapes into the caramel and allow to harden. Eat within a day.

Suggested Wines
Choose a dry white wine, Chablis is particularly suitable, for this menu.

Above: Veal Mornay Below: Salmon Walewska

Here is a menu for a celebration dinner. The menu is planned for 6 people, but would serve 8.

Advance Preparations: A mixed hors d'oeuvre is an excellent start to a meal. It looks colorful, can be prepared beforehand and allows guests to select items they prefer. Mix the oil and vinegar dressing and use as required. Many people have enjoyed Paella in Spain and would be delighted to have it again, so it is a clever choice. It can be partially cooked earlier. The cold Apricot Lemon Soufflé has a sharp refreshing taste which contrasts with the previous courses. There is no need to have a wide range of cheeses after such a satisfying meal, one or two would be quite sufficient. Bunches of carameled grapes are delicious with the coffee.

Preparation of Paella

MIXED HORS D'OEUVRE

Salami Cornets: Twist 12 slices of salami into cones. Slice about 12 small white raw button mushrooms, toss in oil and vinegar, season well. Spoon into the cones, top with halved stuffed olives. Alternatively pipe rosettes of thick mayonnaise and top with olives.

Red Pepper and Cucumber Salad: Blend 3–4 tablespoons diced cucumber with 3–4 tablespoons diced canned red pepper. Toss in well seasoned oil and vinegar.

Carrot Creamed Coleslaw: Blend a little cream and lemon juice into about 4 tablespoons mayonnaise. Toss 6–7½ tablespoons shredded white cabbage and the same amount of coarsely grated carrot with the dressing.

Tomato and Onion Salad: Blend oil and vinegar with seasoning and a pinch of sugar. Cut 1 large onion and 4 tomatoes into rings. Toss in dressing.

Corn Potato Salad: Blend 2½–4 tablespoons mayonnaise with a little oil and vinegar. Blend 3–5 tablespoons cooked or canned sweet corn, 2½–4 tablespoons cooked or canned peas and 6–7½ tablespoons diced cooked or canned potatoes. Toss in the dressing.

Stuffed Egg Mayonnaise: Hard cook 3–4 eggs, halve and remove the yolks. Mash these and blend with 4–5 chopped anchovy fillets. Press into the white cases. Put into a dish, top with mayonnaise flavored with a little ketchup and light cream. Garnish with chopped parsley.

PAELLA

¼ teaspoon saffron powder or few strands saffron ·
3¾ cups chicken stock · 3½–5 tablespoons olive oil ·
2 onions · 1–2 cloves garlic · about 2 pints mussels ·
seasoning · parsley ·
1–1½ lb. diced raw young chicken ·
1 cup long grain rice ·
approximately ½ lb. shelled shrimp ·
few cooked peas

Blend the saffron powder with the stock, or infuse the strands for 30 minutes, then strain. Heat the oil in a large pan and fry the chopped onions and crushed garlic for a few minutes. Meanwhile, put the washed mussels into another pan with enough water to cover. Discard any mussels that do not close when sharply tapped. Add seasoning and a bunch of parsley. Heat until the mussels open. Allow to cool enough to handle, remove most of the mussels from *both* shells, but save a few on halved shells. Add the diced chicken and rice to the onions and garlic, toss in the oily mixture and pour in the saffron-flavored stock. Simmer steadily in an uncovered pan, stirring from time to time, until the rice is almost tender (about 25 minutes). Add the shrimp, peas, mussels and seasoning and complete the cooking.

To vary: Fry 2 skinned, chopped tomatoes with the onion.

APRICOT LEMON SOUFFLÉ

1 large can apricot halves · juice 2 lemons ·
2 envelopes unflavored gelatin · 5 eggs · ¾ cup sugar ·
2 cups heavy cream · chocolate shot

Tie a deep band of buttered waxed paper around the outside of the soufflé dish.

Drain the fruit from the syrup, put 8 halves on one side for decoration. Purée the remaining fruit, add the lemon juice and enough syrup to give 2 cups. Soften the gelatin in a little of the cold apricot mixture. Heat the remainder, stir the softened gelatin into this, and continue stirring until thoroughly dissolved. Separate the egg yolks from the whites. Beat the yolks with the sugar, then beat in the warm apricot mixture. Allow this mixture to cool and begin to stiffen slightly, then fold in 1¼ cups whipped cream and the stiffly beaten egg whites. Spoon into the prepared soufflé dish and leave to set. Remove the band of paper from the mixture and press chocolate shot against the sides. Top with piped heavy cream and the reserved apricots.

Suggested Wines

Serve a dry sherry, dry white wine or Rhine wine with the hors d'oeuvre. A red wine is ideal with the Paella.

Mixed Hors d'Oeuvre, Paella, Apricot Lemon Soufflé

> ## MENU
>
> ### TOMATO AND CELERY SOUP
> ### BEEF SPIRALS WITH PEAS,
> ### CARROTS AND WATERCRESS
> ### APPLE RAISIN MOLD AND
> ### ICE CREAM OR YOGURT

A celebration menu need not be unduly expensive. This menu, for 4 people, is economical and easily prepared. It is also excellent for the 'calorie-conscious'.

Advance Preparations: Make the soup ready to reheat, or serve chilled. Prepare the Beef Spirals, cover until ready to cook, so the meat does not dry. Make the dessert and allow to set; do not keep this longer than 24 hours.

TOMATO AND CELERY SOUP

2 medium-sized onions · 3–4 sticks celery ·
2 tablespoons margarine · 1 lb. tomatoes ·
1¼ cups white stock · seasoning ·
1¼ tablespoons tomato paste ·
Garnish: celery leaves

Chop the onions and celery. Toss in the melted margarine for a few minutes. Add the chopped tomatoes and stock and simmer for 15 minutes. Purée. Return to the pan, heat for a few minutes, then add the seasoning and tomato paste. Pour into soup cups or a tureen. Garnish with chopped celery leaves. This soup is also excellent cold.

Tomato and Celery Soup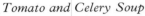

BEEF SPIRALS

1 lb. round steak cut in one piece ·
6 tablespoons butter or margarine ·
2½–4 tablespoons chopped parsley and/or
1 finely chopped green pepper · peas · carrots

Beat the steak until thin. Spread with half the butter or margarine then the chopped parsley and/or the chopped pepper (discard the core and seeds). Roll up like a Swiss roll, cut into 8 slices and secure the spirals with wooden cocktail sticks. Broil or fry in the remaining butter or margarine until tender. Serve in a border of peas and sliced carrots.

APPLE RAISIN MOLD

2 good-sized cooking apples · 1¼ cups water ·
grated rind and juice 1 orange · sugar to taste ·
1 envelope unflavored gelatin ·
2½–4 tablespoons seedless raisins ·
Decoration: fresh orange slices

Simmer the peeled and cored apples with the water, finely grated orange rind and sugar to taste. Purée until smooth. Soften the gelatin in the orange juice. Measure the apple pulp and you should have *nearly* 2½ cups; if insufficient add a little hot water to make the correct amount. Blend the gelatin with the hot apple purée and stir until dissolved. Put the raisins into the bottom of a mold rinsed out in cold water. Spoon over the apple mixture. Leave to set. Turn out, decorate with fresh orange slices and serve with ice cream or yogurt.

Suggested Wines
Choose a red Burgundy or a dry cider for this menu.

Simple Celebration Cake

SIMPLE CELEBRATION CAKE

1 cup margarine or butter · 1 cup sugar · 4 eggs ·
2 cups self-rising flour or all-purpose flour and
2 teaspoons baking powder ·
Icing: 1½ cups butter or margarine ·
3 cups confectioners' sugar ·
finely grated rind 1 orange ·
about 4 tablespoons orange juice ·
few drops yellow or pink coloring

Sometimes one wants a very simple celebration menu; to invite a few friends to 'drop in' for a drink and cake.

Advance Preparations: Cut thin slices of bread and butter, brown or white, and top with smoked salmon; pâté, topped with crisply broiled bacon; inexpensive Danish caviare, topped with hard-cooked egg slices; lightly scrambled egg, topped with shrimp; smoked eel sprinkled with lemon juice; crabmeat mashed with mayonnaise and sprinkled with dill. Cut into small pieces and cover with damp kitchen paper or foil. Make the Celebration Cake 24 hours beforehand.

Cream the margarine or butter with the sugar until soft and light. Add the beaten eggs gradually and then fold in the sifted flour or flour and baking powder. Divide the mixture between two greased and floured 8–9-inch cake pans and bake for approximately 25–30 minutes above the center of a moderate oven, 350–375°F. Turn out carefully and cool. Prepare the icing by creaming the butter or margarine, sugar, orange rind and juice and coloring. Sandwich the cakes together with one quarter of the icing. Coat the sides and top with some of the icing, then tint the remaining icing a slightly deeper color and pipe over the top of the cake. Decorate with a ribbon and candles or a few flowers. Makes 16 small slices.

Gazpacho Garnishes, Ham and Tongue Loaf with Corn Salad, Chocolate Macaroon Trifle

MENU

GAZPACHO
HAM AND TONGUE LOAF
WITH CORN SALAD
CHOCOLATE MACAROON TRIFLE

This menu is an economical one which would be ideal to serve for a formal or buffet meal.

Advance Preparations: All the dishes are prepared beforehand and served cold. Cover the salad with foil.

GAZPACHO
There are many recipes for this excellent chilled tomato and vegetable soup from Spain.

$2\frac{1}{2}$ cups canned tomato juice ·
$1\frac{1}{4}$ tablespoons lemon juice ·
$2\frac{1}{2}$ tablespoons olive oil ·
1–2 crushed cloves garlic ·
1 onion · seasoning ·
Garnish: finely diced cucumber ·
finely diced green pepper · finely diced onion ·
finely diced bread

Blend the tomato juice, lemon juice, olive oil, garlic and finely chopped onion. Season and chill. Serve with the 4 bowls of garnish.

HAM AND TONGUE LOAF

$\frac{1}{2}$ lb. tongue · $\frac{3}{4}$ lb. boiled ham ·
$\frac{2}{3}$ cup fresh breadcrumbs ·
5 tablespoons fresh tomato pulp purée ·
1–$2\frac{1}{2}$ tablespoons chopped parsley · 1 egg · seasoning ·

Garnish: sliced radishes and cucumber

Grind or chop the tongue and ham. Add the breadcrumbs, tomato pulp, chopped parsley, egg and seasoning. Turn into a greased 2 lb. loaf pan, cover with greased foil and bake in the center of a moderate oven, 350–375°F, for about 1 hour. Cool in the pan. Turn out and garnish with radishes and cucumber. Serve with corn salad.

CORN SALAD

about ½ cup cooked or canned sweet corn ·
lettuce · 3 hard-cooked eggs ·
6–8 cold new potatoes · little mayonnaise ·
chopped parsley

Put cooked or canned corn on a bed of lettuce. Garnish with quartered hard-cooked eggs and sliced potatoes. Top with mayonnaise and chopped parsley.

CHOCOLATE MACAROON TRIFLE

6–8 macaroon cookies · 2½ tablespoons rum ·
3¾ tablespoons fresh orange juice · ¼ cup cornstarch ·
2 cups milk · ¼ cup sugar ·
4–6 squares semi-sweet chocolate ·
½ pint heavy cream ·
Topping: whipped cream, few blanched almonds

Put the cookies into a serving dish. Blend the rum with the orange juice. Pour over the cookies. Blend the cornstarch with the milk, add the sugar, and cook gently until thickened. Remove from the heat and add the chocolate, broken into small pieces; stir until dissolved. Stir as the sauce cools and blend with the cream. Pour over the cookies and leave until fairly firm. Top with whipped cream and blanched almonds.

Suggested Wines
Serve a well chilled white Bordeaux (Graves is a good choice).

┌─────────────────────────────┐
│ MENU │
│ │
│ CHEESE AIGRETTES │
│ TROUT NANSEN WITH CUCUMBER SALAD, │
│ ASPARAGUS AND NEW POTATOES │
│ PACIFIC DELIGHT │
└─────────────────────────────┘

Although the main course and the dessert may appear rather ambitious, they are both simple to prepare. This is a frankly luxurious luncheon for 4.

Advance Preparations: I have suggested hot Cheese Aigrettes since the main course is cold and the dessert a combination of hot and cold ingredients. If you do not wish to fry these at the last minute, serve a hot soup, or a pâté, or hot globe artichokes with melted butter (in this case choose another vegetable, *not* asparagus). Prepare the ingredients for the aigrettes; cut the skin from the pineapple and make the main course completely. Make the cucumber salad and cover, prepare the asparagus.

CHEESE AIGRETTES

**2 tablespoons butter or margarine ·
3¾ tablespoons water · ½ cup flour · 2 large eggs ·
6 tablespoons grated Parmesan cheese · seasoning ·
To fry: deep oil ·
Garnish (optional): grated Parmesan, or Parmesan and Cheddar cheese, slivered almonds**

Put the butter or margarine and the water into a pan. Heat until the fat has melted, remove from the heat and stir in the flour. Return to the heat and cook gently for several minutes, until a firm ball. Again remove from the heat and gradually beat in the eggs until a smooth sticky mixture. Add the cheese (do not return to heat), season well. Heat the oil to 350°F (until a tiny piece of the mixture turns golden colored within about a minute). Drop spoonfuls of the mixture into the hot oil, lower the heat and cook for about 7 minutes, turning during cooking. Drain well on absorbent paper. Sprinkle with the garnish if wished. Makes about 16–20.
Note: These can be fried, put on a flat tray in a low oven and kept hot for a *very limited time only*.

TROUT NANSEN

**4 large trout · little seasoning ·
1¼ cups white wine or use half wine and half water ·
½ cup fish stock★ · *bouquet garni* ·
½ package unflavored gelatin ·
2½–4 tablespoons thick mayonnaise ·
little chopped parsley ·
2–3 teaspoons chopped capers ·
1 tablespoon chopped gherkins ·
Garnish: 2 lemons, shelled shrimp, 2 tomatoes,
little cooked or canned asparagus, parsley**
★made by simmering the backbones for a short time or by simmering a small cod's head

Slit the trout along the stomach and carefully remove the backbones (or ask the fishmarket to do this). If using frozen trout allow to defrost, then bone. Try to leave the heads on

Cheese Aigrettes, Trout Nansen, Pacific Delight

the fish as shown in the picture. Wash and dry the fish well, season *very* lightly. Put into a large pan with the wine or wine and water and fish stock. Add the *bouquet garni*, but no more seasoning. Simmer very gently until tender, i.e. about 8–10 minutes. Lift the fish out of the liquid and drain well. Strain the liquid most carefully, measure and if necessary add a little more wine or water to give just *over* 1 cup. Soften the gelatin in a little of the liquid, heat the rest, then add the softened gelatin and stir until dissolved. Put on one side and leave until cool and beginning to stiffen. Meanwhile, blend the mayonnaise, parsley, capers and gherkins and spread a little inside each fish. Put the fish on a serving dish with the sliced lemons and the shrimp. Peel the tomatoes, slice and cut one or two slices into small pieces, put these on the lemon slices. Arrange the rest of the sliced tomatoes and asparagus on the dish, as shown in the picture. Spoon the cold and slightly stiffened gelatin over the fish, garnish and leave until set. Top with parsley.

Cucumber Salad
Peel the cucumber if wished and slice thinly. Top with a little seasoning, lemon juice or white wine vinegar, chopped parsley and chopped chives.

Asparagus
Cut the ends from the asparagus, wash in cold water, tie in bundles and stand in boiling salted water. If you have no asparagus-boiler use the tallest pan possible (I find a deep pressure cooker, used as an ordinary saucepan, excellent). Put a lid on the pan, or cover with foil to retain the steam. Cook for about 12 minutes, until tender. Drain and serve with well-seasoned melted butter.

PACIFIC DELIGHT

**1 ripe medium-sized pineapple · ice cream to serve 4 ·
Meringue: 4 egg whites, ½ cup sugar**

Cut the top from the pineapple very carefully. Put on one side to use for decoration. Cut the pineapple into rings, remove the skin from each slice with a sharp knife or kitchen scissors. Take out the center core with an apple corer. Beat the egg whites until very stiff. Gradually beat in half the sugar then fold in the remainder. Put a slice of pineapple on to an oven-proof serving dish. Fill the center 'hole' with firm ice cream. Top with a second slice of fruit and ice cream, continue like this until the fruit is put together. Put the meringue mixture into a pastry bag fitted with a ¼-inch rose, and pipe to look like the original shape of the pineapple. Put into a very hot oven, 475–500°F, and leave for 3 minutes only, until the meringue is tinged with golden brown. Remove from the oven. Put the leaves on top of the meringue shape and serve. This dessert will stand for 25–30 minutes without the ice cream melting.
Note: When fresh pineapple is not available, use rings of well-drained canned pineapple, in which case use a little less sugar in the meringue.
There is another way to serve this dessert, and that is to peel the pineapple and cut it into slices downwards, removing the hard core. Put a block of ice cream on to the dish, press the slices against the ice cream so it looks like a whole pineapple again, then coat with meringue as above.

Suggested Wines
A well chilled white wine or rosé would blend well with this menu.

```
┌─────────────────────────────────┐
│              MENU               │
│                                 │
│   CHILLED CHICKEN CREAM SOUP    │
│   BEEF AND HAM PÂTÉ LOAF WITH SWEET │
│   AND SOUR ONIONS (see page 44) │
│   CUCUMBER YOGURT SALAD (see page 44) │
│       AND MIXED SALADS          │
│     SPONGE FINGER GÂTEAU        │
│   CHEESE SAVORIES (see page 118)│
└─────────────────────────────────┘
```

This menu is ideal for a hot weather buffet served on your terrace. It serves 10–12.

Advance Preparations: All the dishes are made beforehand.

CHILLED CHICKEN CREAM SOUP

5 cups chicken stock · 2–3 onions or leeks · 2–3 old potatoes · *bouquet garni* · seasoning · about ½ lb. cooked chicken breast · 1¼ cups light cream · chopped chives · chopped parsley

Put the stock into a pan, add the onions or leeks, potatoes, *bouquet garni* and a little seasoning. Simmer for about 20 minutes. Add the chicken and continue cooking for a further 10 minutes. Remove the *bouquet garni*, then purée the mixture in a blender. Add the cream, more seasoning, and a generous amount of chives and parsley. Serve very cold.

BEEF AND HAM PÂTÉ LOAF

1½ lb. round steak · ½–¾ lb. calf's liver · 1 lb. cooked ham · ¼ cup butter or margarine · ½ cup flour · 10 tablespoons brown stock · 1¼ cups milk · 5 tablespoons heavy cream · 2½–4 tablespoons dry sherry · 5 eggs · seasoning · 1–2 teaspoons chopped fresh herbs

Grind the steak, liver and ham very finely. Make a fairly thick sauce with the butter or margarine, flour, stock and milk. Add the cream, sherry, 2 beaten eggs, plenty of seasoning and the herbs. Add all the meats and blend well. Hard-cook the 3 remaining eggs, shell. Put half the meat mixture into a large 2–2½ quart buttered mold, arrange the eggs on this, cover with the rest of the meat mixture, then with well buttered foil or waxed paper. Stand in a tin of cold water and bake for 1½ hours in the center of a moderately low oven, 325°F. Cool in the tin, then turn out just before serving. Serve with salads and mayonnaise.

SPONGE FINGER GÂTEAU

about 30 Lady fingers · 2½ cups heavy cream · sugar to taste · 1½–2 lb. fresh fruit

Put one third of the Lady fingers on a serving dish. Whip the cream, add sugar to taste. Spread some of the cream over the Lady fingers, top with some of the fruit. Add more sponge fingers, more cream and fruit, then a final layer of Lady fingers, cream and fruit. Allow to stand for 1–2 hours before serving.
To vary: Dip the Lady fingers in a little white wine for a few seconds only.

Suggested Wines
Chianti or a light white wine.

```
┌─────────────────────────────────┐
│              MENU               │
│                                 │
│   FRIED SHRIMP AND FRIED CHICKEN│
│      WITH VARIOUS SAUCES        │
│     ORANGES IN RUM SAUCE        │
│   CHEESE SAVORIES (see page 118)│
│         PARTY PUNCH             │
└─────────────────────────────────┘
```

A buffet party menu which would be ideal for hot or cold weather. It serves 10–12 people. If you wanted to serve an hors d'oeuvre, the Creamed Liver Pâté on page 91 would be a good choice.

Advance Preparations: Coat the shrimp and chicken; make the sauces, dessert and cheese savories. The cheese savories can be made several days before and stored in an airtight tin.

FRIED SHRIMP AND FRIED CHICKEN

These two foods may be served together or separately. If you do not know your guests' tastes, it is a good idea to serve them separately as quite a number of people are allergic to shell fish. For a buffet party, cut the chicken into small pieces and remove the bones and skin. Allow 4 shrimp per person plus about 2–3 small pieces of chicken. For about 48 shrimp and 36 pieces of chicken you will need:

4 cups flour · seasoning · 4 eggs · 2½ cups milk · 1¼ cups water · 1 cup flour, seasoned with salt and pepper

Make a batter with the flour, seasoning, eggs, milk and water. Coat the fish and the chicken in seasoned flour, then in batter. Fry shrimp in deep fat for about 2–3 minutes, and chicken about 6–8 minutes. Drain on absorbent paper and serve hot. Obviously if you are frying as large an amount as that suggested above, you will have to keep it warm, so place on flat trays in a low oven.

OLIVE TARTARE SAUCE

2½–4 tablespoons chopped gherkins · 2½–4 tablespoons capers · 2½–4 tablespoons chopped parsley · 2½–4 tablespoons sliced stuffed olives · 1¼ cups mayonnaise · little lemon juice · seasoning

Mix the gherkins, capers, parsley and olives with the mayonnaise. Add the lemon juice and extra seasoning.

SPICED PICKLED CUCUMBER SAUCE

small jar pickled cucumbers · 1–2 teaspoons peppercorns · little mixed spice · 1–2 teaspoons prepared mustard

Chop or slice the cucumbers. Blend the peppercorns, spice and mustard with the liquid from the jar of cucumbers. Put the cucumbers into a dish, pour over the spiced liquid.

HERBED CHUTNEY

Take any sweet chutney, mango, tomato, etc., and blend with finely chopped parsley, chives and any other fresh herbs.

Chilled Chicken Cream Soup, Beef and Ham Pâté Loaf, Salads, Sponge Finger Gâteau

PEPPER SAUCE

1–2 medium-sized green peppers · 1–2 red peppers ·
2½ tablespoons olive oil ·
2½–4 tablespoons white malt or wine vinegar ·
1 teaspoon prepared mustard · 1 teaspoon sugar ·
1–2 teaspoons peppercorns or very good shake black
pepper and salt ·
1–2½ tablespoons raisins (optional)

Chop the green and red peppers, discarding the cores and
seeds; use canned red peppers if the fresh are not available.
Blend the olive oil, vinegar, mustard, sugar and peppercorns
or pepper and salt. Pour over the mixed peppers and allow to
stand for about 1 hour. Add the raisins just before serving if
wished.

ORANGES IN RUM SAUCE

12 medium-sized oranges · 1¼ cups water ·
1 cup sugar · 5–6 tablespoons rum

Cut away the peel from the oranges, removing all the pith as
well. Cut the orange part of some of the peel into very narrow

strips, as shown in the picture. Soak in half the water for
1 hour, then simmer in this water in a covered pan for about
20 minutes. Stand in the liquid until ready to add to the
caramel. Put the sugar and the remaining water into a strong
pan. Stir over a low heat until the sugar dissolves, then boil
steadily, without stirring, until the mixture turns golden
brown. Strain liquid from the orange peel into the caramel,
stir over the heat until blended, then add the rum. Put the
oranges into a dish, pour the syrup over slowly so it soaks
into the fruit and top with the peel.

PARTY PUNCH

2 bottles rosé wine · about 2½ cups soda water ·
2 glasses brandy

Blend the wine with the soda water and brandy. *If wishing to
serve as a hot punch:* Heat with 2½–4 tablespoons sugar and
the juice of 1–2 lemons. Top with lemon slices. *If wishing to
serve cold:* I do not add sugar or lemon juice, but just pour the
wine, soda and brandy mixture over a little crushed ice and
decorate with slices of lemon and mint. Makes about 12–16
glasses.

Oranges in Rum Sauce

This menu would appeal to young people. It serves 10–12. Serve with cider, beer or soft drinks rather than wine.

Advance Preparations: Make the dip and prepare the tray of foods around it. Partially cook the Kedgeree and just reheat; prepare the Shish-Kebabs.

AVOCADO DIP (GUACOMOLE)

2 large avocados · 3 large tomatoes · 1 small onion · ½ cup sour cream · 1¼ tablespoons lemon juice · 3¾ tablespoons mayonnaise · seasoning · few drops Tabasco sauce

Halve the avocados, remove the flesh and mash. Add the remaining ingredients. Serve with potato chips, raw vegetables and crackers.

KEDGEREE

½ cup butter or margarine · 3 cups cooked rice · 1½ lb. cooked smoked haddock · 10 tablespoons light cream · 3–4 hard-cooked eggs · seasoning

Heat the butter or margarine in a pan. Add the rice, flaked haddock and cream. Heat gently, then add the chopped egg whites and seasoning. Top with the chopped egg yolks.

SHISH-KEBABS

Put cubes of tender lamb, rolled in seasoning and a little chopped fresh rosemary, on to metal skewers, with rings of cucumber and/or rings of green pepper and/or slices of lemon. You can also add small mushrooms, tomatoes and tiny onions (par-boil these first). Brush with oil or melted butter and broil until tender. Serve with various sauces; those on page 108 would be excellent.

Avocado Dip (Guacamole)

One of the easiest, and most enjoyable, of buffet-type parties is to serve a variety of cheeses with suitable wines.

If you are expecting rather a large number of guests and have relatively little space in which to entertain them, dice the cheese beforehand, so it is easier to serve. The cheese looks more inviting, in this case, if the cubes are placed on cocktail sticks and speared into red and/or green cabbages and grapefruit. Obviously cheese that crumbles easily, such as mature Danish Blue and Roquefort, cannot be served in this way and should be arranged in bowls or on dishes with colorful garnishes. The usual arrangement, though, is to have several cheese boards on the table, each one containing a selection of cheese and garnished with bunches of grapes, orange segments, radishes, celery, etc., so your guests may then help themselves.

Cheeses to Choose

It is wise to 'play for safety' by having some well known, also much liked, Cheddar cheese. If you have this, then choose either Cheshire or imported Swiss as a second firm cheese. Have a full-flavored cheese, such as Danish Blue, Roquefort, Stilton or Gorgonzola.

Choose a 'creamy' type cheese with plenty of flavor such as a Brie, Camembert or Pont l'Eveque and a really creamy cheese such as Bel Paese, or a local cream cheese.

Many people today are calorie-conscious so have bowls of low-calorie cottage cheese. As this is very colorless you may like to mix it with chopped fresh fruit.

The above are basic ideas; there is such a variety of cheeses from which to choose that your Cheese Party need never be dull.

Some extra cheeses I personally would include would be a smoked cheese, a Port du Salut, a very good Caerphilly and a Boursin.

If your party includes children, then the milder processed cheeses might well be popular.

The suggested wines are given below. If you wish to provide just a choice of one red and one white or rosé (and this is

certainly easier for serving), then I would choose the wines that come at the beginning of the lists. On the other hand, it is enjoyable for your guests to sample a variety of wines on such an occasion.

Suggested Wines

Red Wines
Mouton-Cadet, Médoc, St. Emilion, Nuits St. Georges, Gevrey-Chambertin, Volnay, an Italian Valpolicella or, of course, any of the delicious California wines.

White Wines
Pouilly-Fuissé, or better still if you like an interesting flavor, a Pouilly-Fumée, Puligny-Montrachet or some of the German wines – Liebfraumilch is one of the most popular. Try also Riesling, a Soave di Verona from Italy or, of course, a nice California Chablis.

Rosé Wines
The best known Portuguese Mateus Rosé blends well with many cheeses, but less hackneyed is the French Tavel rosé or Beaujolais rosé or a really dry Pradei rosé or even an Anjou rosé.

Many people might enjoy a beer, lager or cider with cheese. Serve white and rosé wines well chilled, red wines at room temperature.

Some of the best accompaniments to cheese will be crusty French bread or crisp rolls. Have crispbreads, various crackers and fingers of a rich fruit cake (or tiny hot mince pies) to blend with the creamy cheese. Include plenty of salads and fruit, too. The fruits I would choose would be fingers of ripe melon, crisp apples, firm but ripe pears and cherries when in season.

Quantities to Allow
Allow $\frac{1}{4}-\frac{1}{2}$ lb. cheese per person – buy generously, for the cheese will keep – and 3 rolls or the equivalent in bread with several crackers or crisbreads per person plus about $\frac{1}{4}$ cup butter per person.
If you allow $\frac{1}{2}$ bottle of wine per person that should be sufficient.
Coffee will also be appreciated so allow 2 cups of coffee per person.

MENU

OPEN SANDWICHES
SAUSAGES ON STICKS,
SAUSAGE ROLLS OR HAMBURGERS
POTATO CHIPS
CHEESE AND CARROT DIP
ICED RABBIT COOKIES
BABY MERINGUES
BIRTHDAY CAKE
ICE CREAM
JELLO
MILK SHAKES (see page 73)
OR
LEMONADE (see page 70)

Advance Preparations: All the food can be prepared in advance. The sausage rolls and hamburgers can just be reheated.

OPEN SANDWICHES

Finger rolls · butter or margarine ·
toppings (see method)

Split the rolls, spread with butter and then with the topping.

TOPPINGS

Scrambled eggs; cream cheese spread (or a not too rich cream cheese); yeast extract; ham; potted meat and potted fish. Garnish with cooked well drained prunes, mandarin orange segments or tomato slices. Mashed banana (with a little sugar and lemon juice); honey; jam; peanut butter and nuts. Decorate with prunes, halved dates or apple slices.

SAUSAGES ON STICKS

If you cannot buy small cocktail sausages, twist pork sausages in half and then cut through to give 2 sausages. Broil; fry or bake in the oven until brown; drain on absorbent paper.

Reheat as required or serve cold.

CHEESE AND CARROT DIP

1 lb. Cheddar cheese · ½ cup light cream ·
1–2½ tablespoons mayonnaise · 2–3 firm carrots

Grate the cheese finely and blend with cream to make a consistency like heavy cream, then add a little mayonnaise to make a more piquant flavor. Grate the carrots finely, stir most of the carrot into the cheese mixture. Spoon into a dish and top with the rest of the carrot. Serve on a large plate with potato chips and sausages as 'dips'. Serves about 12.

ICED RABBIT COOKIES

¾ cup margarine · ¾ cup sugar · 3 cups flour ·
little milk or egg ·
Decoration: 1½ cups confectioners' sugar ·
little orange juice · coloring · currants

Cream the margarine and sugar, add the flour and just enough milk or egg to make a firm rolling consistency. Knead well, roll out on a lightly floured board and cut into 'rabbit' shapes, either using a metal cutter or cutting round a cardboard shape. Save enough dough to cut oblong pieces, upon which the 'rabbits' will stand when baked and iced. Put on to ungreased cookie trays, bake for 12–15 minutes in the center of a very moderate oven, 325–350°F. Cool on the trays and store until ready to serve. Blend the confectioners' sugar with orange juice and coloring, ice the 'stands' and the 'rabbits', press currants in position for 'eyes'. (The cookies may be served without icing.) Makes about 16.

SAUSAGE ROLLS

Flaky pastry: 4 cups flour · pinch salt ·
1½ cups margarine or a mixture of margarine and shortening or butter · water to bind ·
1½ lb. sausagemeat · 2 eggs

Flaky pastry is better for children, as it is less rich than puff pastry. Sift the flour and salt, rub in one-third of the margarine or mixed fats and bind with water to an elastic rolling

Cheese and Carrot Dip, Iced Rabbit Cookies, Baby Meringues, Open Sandwiches, Birthday Cake

Hamburgers

consistency. Roll out to an oblong shape. Divide the re-remaining fat in half, then into tiny pieces. Cover two-thirds of the dough with half the fat, fold like an envelope, turn at right angles, seal the edges, 'rib' the pastry (i.e., depress at regular intervals). Roll out and repeat with the rest of the fat, fold, turn at right angles, seal the edges and put into a cool place until ready to use.

Make the sausagemeat into long strips, about the thickness of a large cigar. Roll out the pastry and cut into strips, sufficiently wide to cover the sausagemeat. Put the strips of sausagemeat on the strips of pastry. Brush the edges with water, seal firmly and flake with the edge of a knife. Cut into pieces about 1½ inches long and make 2–3 slits on top. Beat the eggs with a little water, brush over the sausage rolls and bake on an ungreased cookie tray for about 12 minutes in the center of a very hot oven, 450–475°F, then lower the heat to moderate and cook for another 5–6 minutes. Serve hot or cold. Makes 36 rolls; allow 2–3 per person.

HAMBURGERS

2 lb. ground beef · 2 eggs or 4 egg yolks · seasoning · pinch mixed herbs · flour · fat for frying · rolls

Mix the meat, eggs or egg yolks, seasoning and herbs together and form into about 24 small flat cakes. If you flour your hands you can handle the meat mixture more easily. Fry in a little hot fat for about 3 minutes on either side or bake on well greased cookie trays for about 12 minutes in a hot oven. Serve on small toasted round rolls. Makes about 24.

BABY MERINGUES

**White meringues: 2 egg whites · ½ cup sugar ·
Chocolate meringues: 2 egg whites · ½ cup sugar ·
2½ tablespoons cocoa**

Beat the egg whites until stiff. Beat in half the sugar then fold in the remainder. When making the chocolate meringues blend the cocoa with the sugar. Pipe into rose shapes on lightly oiled cookie trays and dry out for approximately 1½ hours in the coolest part of a very slow oven, 250–275°F. Lift off the trays while warm, cool, then store in an airtight tin until ready to serve. They can be served plain or sandwiched together with whipped cream. This makes about 36.

BIRTHDAY CAKE

Make a cake (see page 103) using 1 cup margarine, etc., then sandwich together and decorate with butter icing and a chocolate figure as in the picture. Tie a band of ribbon around the outside of the cake. This makes about 14–16 slices.

NEW WAYS TO SERVE JELLO

Make up fruit-flavored gelatin and:
Beat and fill ice cream cones.
Beat and put on to saucers, top with pear 'mice'.
Cut a slice from oranges, squeeze out the juice and use this to make the gelatin (adding water to bring up to the full quantity). Remove the pith and fill the orange cases with the cool gelatin. When set put 'lids' in position.

Cocktail Parties

This is an ideal way to entertain a large number of people, either at noon or early in the evening. The drinks can be as varied as you wish. The food can be simple or original and hot or cold. A good selection of hors d'oeuvres will be appreciated by your guests.

```
MENU

HORS D'OEUVRES
GHERKINS
OLIVES
CHIPS
NUTS
```

Allow 6–7 hors d'oeuvres per person plus nuts and potato chips.

Advance Preparations: All the dishes can be prepared beforehand.

CHEESE PASTRY

This pastry is not only used for cheese straws and other cheese cookies, but it can be used for tiny tartlet cases instead of short crust pastry.

2 cups flour · good pinch salt · shake pepper ·
shake cayenne pepper · pinch dry mustard ·
½ cup butter, margarine or shortening ·
¾ cup grated Parmesan cheese · 2 egg yolks ·
water to mix

Sift the dry ingredients together. Rub the butter, margarine or shortening into the flour. Add the cheese, then the egg yolks and sufficient water to make a rolling consistency. Roll out and use as the individual recipes. You can make a batch of pastry and use it for several recipes. Cook as the individual recipes.

CHEESE SAVORIES

All these savories are based upon the quantities given for the Cheese Pastry (above). If you are planning to entertain a number of friends make up 3 or 4 times the amount given and produce a selection of cheese savories. These can be served with cocktails or as a savory for a buffet or dinner party.

Cheese Straws: Roll out the pastry until one-third of an inch in thickness. Cut into narrow fingers, put on to well greased cookie trays. Save a little pastry to make rings. Brush straws and rings with egg white and bake for 8–10

minutes towards the top of a hot oven, 425–450°F. Cool on the trays, then lift off carefully and store in an airtight tin. Put some of the straws through the rings to serve. Makes about 60 straws and 8–10 rings.

Cheese Twists: Roll out the cheese pastry, spread half with grated cheese or chopped nuts, top with the remaining pastry. Cut into thin strips and twist. Bake as cheese straws (above). Makes about 60.

Curried Patties: Roll out the pastry and cut into about 28–30 cocktail-sized rounds or 12–14 larger sized rounds. Grind ½ lb. lean ham, blend with 1–2½ tablespoons flaked coconut, 1 tablespoon white raisins and a little chopped parsley. Put into the center of the rounds. Brush the edges with water, fold over and seal. Bake for 15 minutes in the center of a moderate to moderately hot oven, 375–400°F. Makes 28–30 patties.

COCKTAIL QUICHE LORRAINE

short crust or cheese pastry (see page 71 or above) ·
4–6 slices bacon · 3 eggs · seasoning ·
¾ cup grated Parmesan cheese · 2 cups milk

Line small cocktail-sized tartlet tins with short crust or cheese pastry. The quantity of cheese pastry above lines about 36 tartlet cases. If using short crust pastry, you need 2½ cups flour, etc., to line the same number of tins. Fry the bacon lightly, then chop finely and divide between the tartlets. Beat the eggs with the seasoning, cheese and milk. Spoon into the uncooked pastry cases, bake for 7–8 minutes in the center of a moderately hot to hot oven, 400–425°F. Lower the heat to very moderate and bake for a further 10–15 minutes. Makes about 36.

AVOCADO TARTLETS

cheese pastry (see above) · 1–2 egg whites ·
Filling: 2 large ripe avocados ·
2½ tablespoons lemon juice ·
2½ tablespoons thick mayonnaise ·
2½–4 tablespoons whipped cream or
soft cream cheese · seasoning ·
Garnish: watercress

Make the pastry. Roll out thinly, cut into rounds and line

Making Cheese Pastry

36 tiny cocktail tartlet tins. Prick the base of the tarts with a fork, brush with egg white to give a shine and bake as the Cheese Straws (above). Allow to cool. Do *not* fill until just before serving. Halve the avocados, remove the pulp, mash with the lemon juice and mayonnaise and blend with the cream or cream cheese, season. Spoon into the tartlet cases and top with watercress leaves. These small tartlet cases may be cooked earlier and stored until ready to fill.

To vary: Make a smaller amount of the avocado mixture, fill half the tartlet cases, then fill the rest with scrambled eggs and chopped shrimp, flaked cooked or canned salmon and mayonnaise or chopped ham blended with cream cheese and mayonnaise.

CANAPÉS

Base: These can be rounds of buttered bread, toast, pastry, fried bread (well drained), tiny plain crackers or rounds of cheese pastry (baked as Cheese Straws, page 118).

Anchovy and Egg Canapés: Hard-cook 2 eggs, remove the yolks and mash with $\frac{1}{4}$ cup butter, anchovy extract and a shake of pepper. Pipe on to the base and top with sliced stuffed olives or pieces of cheese. Makes 20.

Asparagus Rolls: Spread thin slices of brown bread and butter with cream cheese or thick mayonnaise and roll round asparagus tips. If you roll the bread slices with a rolling pin they are more pliable.

Caviar Canapés: Top rounds of brown bread and butter with slices of hard-cooked egg and caviar. If you blend the caviar with a little heavy cream and lemon juice it is softer and easier to spread.

Cheese Bites: Cut neat pieces of slightly under-ripe Danish Blue cheese, Cheddar, Cheshire or other firm cheese. Top with pineapple pieces, then glacé or Maraschino cherries, or with grapes or halved walnuts. Put on cocktail sticks.

Cheese Whirls: Blend cream cheese mixed with butter, mayonnaise or sour cream to make a piping consistency. Pipe on to the base. Sprinkle with paprika.

Christmas Menus

Most families like a traditional meal at Christmas, with turkey or goose as the main dish, followed by Christmas pudding.

MENU

MELON OR SOUP
ROAST TURKEY WITH STUFFINGS
SAUSAGES
ROAST POTATOES
BREAD AND CRANBERRY SAUCES
CHRISTMAS PUDDING
BRANDY BUTTER
MINCE PIES
CHEESE TRAY

This menu would serve 10–12 people with plenty of turkey left over to serve cold.

Advance Preparations: Make the stuffings for the turkey (these can be frozen if wished). Prepare the crumbs for the bread sauce; this also can be frozen and so can the cranberry sauce.

Cook the Christmas pudding some weeks before Christmas. Make the brandy butter and mince pies a day or so beforehand (although both freeze well).

ROAST TURKEY

18 lb. turkey (weight when trussed) ·
$\frac{1}{2}$ cup butter or about 1 cup fat bacon ·
Chestnut Stuffing: 1 lb. chestnuts ·
$1\frac{1}{4}$ cups ham or turkey stock · $\frac{1}{4}$ lb. ham ·
$\frac{1}{2}$ lb. pork sausagemeat · seasoning ·
little extra stock ·
Parsley and Thyme Stuffing:
$2\frac{1}{2}$ cups fresh breadcrumbs ·
4–5 tablespoons chopped parsley ·
grated rind and juice 2 lemons ·
$\frac{1}{2}$ cup shredded suet or melted margarine or butter ·
$\frac{1}{2}$–1 tablespoon chopped fresh thyme ·
seasoning · 2 eggs

When calculating the weight of the turkey and cooking time, include the weight of the stuffings as well. Put the stuffings at either end of the turkey and cover with the butter or bacon. Allow 15 minutes per lb. and 15 minutes over for a bird up to 12 lb. in weight; after this add an additional 12 minutes per lb. up to 21 lb.; after this 10 minutes only for each

additional 1 lb. If the bird is exceptionally broad-breasted, allow a little extra cooking time; so the 18 lb. turkey plus the stuffings would need a total of nearly 5 hours. Set the oven to hot, 425–450°F, then after the first 30–40 minutes lower the heat to moderately hot, approximately 400°F. Remember, if using a covered roasting pan or wrapping the bird in foil, that you should add an additional 20 minutes' cooking time. Time the cooking so that the turkey comes out of the oven about 8–10 minutes before you wish to carve it; this short 'rest' allows the flesh to set a little and makes it easier to carve. Put sausages into the oven about 45 minutes before the end of the cooking time and potatoes to roast about 1 hour before the end of the cooking time.

CHESTNUT STUFFING

Slit the chestnut skins and boil in water for 5–10 minutes, then remove the skins while hot. Put the chestnuts into the stock and simmer until tender and most of the stock has been absorbed. Purée and mix with the chopped ham, sausagemeat, seasoning and enough stock to give a moist mixture.

PARSLEY AND THYME STUFFING

Mix the breadcrumbs with the parsley, grated lemon rind, suet, margarine or butter, thyme, seasoning, lemon juice and eggs.

BREAD SAUCE

2 cups fresh breadcrumbs · $2\frac{1}{2}$ cups milk ·
2 tablespoons butter ·
1 onion (stuck with cloves if wished) · seasoning ·
6–$7\frac{1}{2}$ tablespoons heavy cream

Put all the ingredients into a pan, bring to the boil then leave to infuse over a pan of hot water. Heat, stirring well, just before the meal and remove the onion.

CRANBERRY SAUCE

$1\frac{1}{4}$ cups water · $\frac{1}{2}$ cup sugar · 1 lb. cranberries ·
$2\frac{1}{2}$ tablespoons port wine

The Christmas Dinner

Make a syrup of the water and sugar. Add the cranberries and simmer steadily until tender. Purée to make a smooth mixture and blend with the port wine. If preferred, keep whole.

FEATHER-LIGHT CHRISTMAS PUDDING

**2½ cups seedless raisins · ½ cup white raisins ·
½ cup currants · 3¾ tablespoons dry sherry ·
5 tablespoons orange juice · grated rind 2 oranges ·
grated rind 1 lemon · 2½ tablespoons marmalade ·
¾ cup margarine or butter · 1 cup moist brown sugar ·
3 eggs · 2 cups fresh breadcrumbs · 1½ cups flour ·
1 teaspoon mixed spice · 2½ tablespoons lemon juice**

This pudding can be made several weeks before Christmas, but if you have left it until near the day, it is an excellent choice since it does not require time to mature. Put the dried fruits with the sherry and orange juice into a bowl and leave for 1 hour. Cream the orange and lemon rinds, marmalade, margarine or butter and sugar until soft. Gradually beat in the eggs, then add the crumbs, the flour sifted with the spice, and the lemon juice. Lastly add the fruit with all the moisture. Put into a 2 quart well-greased bowl, press down firmly, cover with greased waxed paper and foil and steam for 3–4 hours. Remove the damp covers, put on dry covers and store in a cool place. Steam for 2 hours on Christmas Day.

To vary: Traditional rich dark pudding: Use another ½ cup white raisins and another ½ cup currants. Use stout instead of orange juice and shredded suet in place of margarine or butter. Add ¾ cup chopped candied peel, a small grated carrot, a small grated apple and ½ cup chopped blanched almonds. Add ½–1 teaspoon ground cinnamon. Steam for 4–5 hours then a further 2–3 hours on Christmas Day.

BRANDY BUTTER (HARD SAUCE)

**1 cup unsalted butter ·
3 cups sifted confectioners' sugar · ½ cup brandy ·
blanched almonds and cherries (optional)**

Roast Goose

Cream the butter and sugar, then gradually work in the brandy. Pile or pipe into a dish and top with almonds and cherries, if wished. Chill well. Serves up to 16.

MINCE PIES

These can be made with short crust pastry, sweet short crust, flaky or puff pastry. Short crust pastry made with 4 cups flour, etc., will give 24–30 individual mince pies.
Roll out the pastry fairly thinly. Cut just over half the pastry into rounds and put into fairly deep tart pans. Fill with mincemeat. Damp the edges of the pastry. Cut out smaller rounds with the remaining pastry, press on top of the filling. Seal the edges, make 2 slits on top to allow the steam to escape. Bake for approximately 15–20 minutes in the center of a hot oven, 425°F, until pale golden and firm. Dust with sifted confectioners' sugar or granulated sugar.

HOME-MADE MINCEMEAT

Home-made mincemeat is very easy to make. As it requires no cooking (except when put into mince pies or other dishes) do not cut down on the amount of sugar and whiskey or other alcohol.

**1 cup currants · ¾ cup seedless chopped raisins ·
½ cup white raisins · 1 peeled, cored, grated apple ·
¾ cup brown sugar ·
½ cup melted margarine or butter ·
¾ cup finely chopped candied peel ·
½ cup finely chopped blanched almonds ·
1 teaspoon mixed spice · 1 teaspoon grated nutmeg ·
5 tablespoons whiskey, brandy or rum ·
grated rind and juice 1 lemon**

Mix all the ingredients together, put into jars, seal down and keep in a cool dry place.

Suggested Drinks

As Christmas celebrations are shared by all ages it is wise to have a selection of alcoholic and soft drinks.

Fresh Fruit Salad

Since goose is large-boned poultry, with little meat on the breast, a bird weighing about 12 lb. will serve only 8 people or even less.

Advance Preparations: As Menu on page 122.

ROAST GOOSE

The oven temperature is the same as for roast turkey, page 122. Do not use any form of fat over the bird. The important point is to make sure the excess fat runs out of the bird. It is quite a good idea to put the goose on a rack in the roasting pan or to pour away the surplus fat during cooking. Follow the timing for roast turkey on page 122. Prick the skin of the goose several times during cooking to allow the fat to 'spurt out'. Do this *lightly* – if you prick too hard there is a tendency for the fat to run *into* the flesh. Serve roast goose, as roast turkey, with thickened gravy made by obtaining a good stock from the giblets of the bird. The recipe for apple sauce is given on page 54.

SAGE AND ONION STUFFING

4 large onions · seasoning · 1¼ cups water ·
2 cups fresh breadcrumbs ·
½–1 tablespoon chopped sage or 1 teaspoon dried sage ·
½ cup melted margarine · 1–2 eggs (optional)

Peel and chop the onions and simmer in the well-seasoned water for 10 minutes. Strain and blend with the remaining ingredients. Bind with an egg and stock, the 2 eggs or all onion stock. Put into the goose.

FRESH FRUIT SALAD

1½ cups water · 2 oranges · 1 lemon · ½ cup sugar ·
2 lb. mixed prepared fresh fruit

Put the water, with *thin* strips of orange and lemon rind, into a pan. Take just the top 'zest' from the fruit. Simmer for 5 minutes. Add the sugar, stir until dissolved then add the orange and lemon juice. Strain over the prepared fruit, allow to become cold.
To vary: Add a little sherry, kirsch, Cointreau or Maraschino to the syrup. Use all fresh orange and lemon juice, omit the water and sugar.
Serve with cream.

125

Index

ACKNOWLEDGEMENTS

The publishers would like to acknowledge the help of the following in providing photographs for this book: National Dairy Council: Peach and Cherry Trifle page 14, Banana and Lemon Cream page 34; Pasta Foods Ltd: Mexican Frankfurters page 44; RHM Foods Ltd: Mexican Macaroni page 30; Syndication International: Cauliflower Surprise page 47, Fruit Meringue Trifle page 79, composite photographs on pages 72, 109. The publishers would like to acknowledge the help of the following for their loan of accessories for photography:
Below Stairs, 212 Upper Richmond Road, London S.W. 14: pine furniture for cover photograph; Carrier Cookshops, 82 Pimlico Road, London S.W. 1: pages 17, 37, 43, 61, 65; Casa Pupo, 56 Pimlico Road, London S.W. 1: pages 23, 40, 81; Craftsmen Potters' Association, Marshall Street, London W. 1: page 53; Crocks Reject China, Richmond Bridge, Richmond, Surrey: china for cover photograph also pages 2, 3, 10, 17, 48, 49, 111; Danasco Ltd, Chelsea Manor Gardens, London S.W. 3: china for cover photograph; Elizabeth David, 46 Bourne Street, London S.W. 1: pages 31, 33; Garrard, 112 Regent Street, London W. 1: page 106; Wedgwood from Gered, Piccadilly, Regent Street, London W. 1: pages 46, 85; Heal's Ltd., 196 Tottenham Court Road, London W. 1: china for cover photograph; Robert Jackson & Co., 172 Piccadily, London W. 1: pages 8, 21, 86, 88, 104; David Mellor Ironmonger, 4 Sloane Square, London S.W. 1: pages 20, 22, 51, 78, 101, 117 also cutlery in most of the photographs; Harvey Nichols, Knightsbridge, London S.W. 1: pages 11, 31, 38, 40, 43, 102, 103, 114; Rosenthal Studio House Ltd: 102 Brompton Road, London S.W. 1: pages 15, 39, Wilson & Gill, 37 Regent Street, London W. 1: page 99.